THIS PAGE:
Padre Island National Seashore is home to a variety of sea turtles. The Kemp's ridley sea turtle (pictured) is the smallest. Radio transmitters help researchers track turtle populations.

ON THE COVER:
Dunes on Padre Island National Seashore. The park was established to preserve one of the last undeveloped barrier islands in the United States.

National Park Service photographs by Rebecca Beavers (NPS Geologic Resources Division).

Padre Island National Seashore

Geologic Resources Inventory Report

Natural Resource Report NPS/NRPC/GRD/NRR—2010/246

Geologic Resources Division
Natural Resource Program Center
P.O. Box 25287
Denver, Colorado 80225

September 2010

U.S. Department of the Interior
National Park Service
Natural Resource Program Center
Ft. Collins, Colorado

The National Park Service, Natural Resource Program Center publishes a range of reports that address natural resource topics of interest and applicability to a broad audience in the National Park Service and others in natural resource management, including scientists, conservation and environmental constituencies, and the public.

The Natural Resource Report Series is used to disseminate high-priority, current natural resource management information with managerial application. The series targets a general, diverse audience, and may contain NPS policy considerations or address sensitive issues of management applicability.

All manuscripts in the series receive the appropriate level of peer review to ensure that the information is scientifically credible, technically accurate, appropriately written for the intended audience, and designed and published in a professional manner. This report received informal peer review by subject-matter experts who were not directly involved in the collection, analysis, or reporting of the data.

Views, statements, findings, conclusions, recommendations, and data in this report do not necessarily reflect views and policies of the National Park Service, U.S. Department of the Interior. Mention of trade names or commercial products does not constitute endorsement or recommendation for use by the U. S. Government.

Printed copies of this report are produced in a limited quantity and they are only available as long as the supply lasts. This report is available from the Geologic Resources Inventory website (http://www.nature.nps.gov/geology/inventory/gre_publications.cfm) and the Natural Resource Publications Management website (http://www.nature.nps.gov/publications/NRPM).

Please cite this publication as:

KellerLynn, K. 2010. Padre Island National Seashore: geologic resources inventory report. Natural Resource Report NPS/NRPC/GRD/NRR—2010/246. National Park Service, Ft. Collins, Colorado.

Contents

List of Figures

List of Tables

Executive Summary

This report accompanies the digital geologic map data for Padre Island National Seashore in Texas, produced by the Geologic Resources Division in collaboration with its partners. It contains information relevant to resource management and scientific research. This document incorporates preexisting geologic information and does not include new data or additional fieldwork.

In 1962 Congress established a national seashore on Padre Island to save a part of the United States shoreline from development. Bounded by the Gulf of Mexico to the east and Laguna Madre to the west, Padre Island National Seashore preserves a barrier island–lagoon system, including the nearshore zone; sandy and shelly beaches; active and stabilized dunes; barrier flats with ponds, marshes, and wind-deflation troughs; wind-tidal flats; grassflats; sand and shell islands; and a hypersaline estuary. Padre Island National Seashore's enabling legislation intends for the seashore's resources to be enjoyed by the public, and more than 642,000 visitors were drawn to its beaches and estuary in 2009.

The dominant shoreline process at the national seashore is wind, which creates waves that drive currents, which in turn transport sediment. The wind shapes both the fore-island dunes and the back-island landscapes. Converging currents around latitude 27°N influence barrier-island development, determine the character of the beaches. Astronomical tides (produced by the gravitational pull of the moon and sun) are minor compared to meteorological (wind-induced) tides, which have a much greater effect on the geomorphic processes and landscapes of Padre Island National Seashore.

Geologic issues that may require management attention include the following:

- Coastal vulnerability. Based on six variables—geomorphology, shoreline change (erosion/accretion), regional coastal slope, relative sea-level change, mean significant wave height, and mean tidal range—investigators determined that 17% of the Gulf of Mexico shoreline at Padre Island National Seashore has very high vulnerability to future sea-level rise; 28% has high vulnerability; 29% has moderate vulnerability; and 26% has low vulnerability. The most vulnerable segment of the shoreline is in the southern part of the national seashore.

- Blowing sand. Blowing sand is ubiquitous at Padre Island National Seashore. Bulldozers continually scrape windblown sand off paved parking lots. Tongues of sand creep relentlessly onto park roads. Windblown sand repeatedly engulfs the patrol cabin at milepost 42. However, the area of greatest management concern regarding blowing sand is at the Malaquite Beach area, which has a long history of anthropogenic impacts, including removal of the fore-island dunes.

- Hurricanes. Hurricanes periodically make landfall in the vicinity of Padre Island National Seashore.

Hurricanes cause severe erosion, particularly in the southern part of the national seashore, where storm washover channels are numerous. Washover channels eroded during past hurricanes are likely to be reactivated during future storms. These storms also cause deposition on the lagoon side of the island, creating important substrate for seagrass, marshes, and sand flats.

- Benthic habitat mapping. Padre Island National Seashore contains 42 km² (16 mi²) of marine resources. This offshore region is known only generally because the benthic environment has not been mapped. Mapping of this area would clarify the land-water interface; relationships of marine features to terrestrial ones; bathymetric features, such as navigation hazards; seafloor features that influence waves, currents, and storm surge; the areal extent and health of marine resources; and sediment characterization and quality as habitat.

- Bird Island Basin. Bird Island Basin encompasses 486 ha (1,200 ac) of barrier-island and lagoonal environments. As a result of its high visitor use and the variety and density of recreational activities in the area, all the geologic processes requiring management attention in Bird Island Basin have a human component. These processes are (1) shoreline erosion, (2) infilling/sedimentation of the boat basin, (3) erosion via runoff, and (4) reduction in sand supply and renourishment.

- Vehicle impacts. Most of the national seashore's beaches are open to motor vehicles and motorcycles. Various studies have investigated recreational impacts and found that beach driving inhibits the development of coppice dunes on the back beach, tending to make the beach zone wider while also inhibiting accretion and decreasing the overall width of the barrier island. Beach driving changes the water-holding capacity of beach sediments, increases shoreline erosion and instability during storms, eliminates the natural rebuilding capacity of the foredune system between storms, and changes dune forms and creates blowouts by destroying vegetation that stabilizes dunes.

- Dredging. In the vicinity of Padre Island National Seashore, one artificial pass (Mansfield Channel) and one artificial waterway (Gulf Intracoastal Waterway) require maintenance dredging to remain open to boat traffic. Yarborough Pass is a "failed" channel through the island. The effects of dredging and disposal of dredge material are primary management concerns, particularly because they affect Laguna Madre's biological productivity, grassflats, and bird populations.

- Oil and gas operations. Oil and gas activity currently consists of 8 pipelines, covering a total of 108 km (67 mi); 14 active wells (13 gas, 1 water); 5 permitted wells; and 172 ha (425 ac) of surface disturbance. Although oil and gas activities in the Gulf of Mexico can impact park resources, the greatest threats are from accidental leaks and spills of hydrocarbons from pipelines and producing wells within the national seashore.

- Shoreline debris. Geologic processes (i.e., converging currents) drive deposition of natural (i.e., sand and shell) and unnatural (shoreline trash) objects onto the shores of Padre Island National Seashore. In an attempt to clean the beaches of trash, many coastal communities spend millions of dollars each year and conduct volunteer clean-ups. Such measures, however, resolve the problem only temporarily, and trash usually reappears on the shoreline within a short time. A 10-year (1989–1998) study at Padre Island National Seashore established protocols and methods and compiled a baseline inventory of shoreline debris. Current park managers could build on this study in order to identify point sources and develop outreach efforts to reduce the amount of trash that washes ashore.

- Grazing. Padre Island's coastal prairies, absence of chaparral, and natural boundaries for containing cattle made it an ideal location for cattle operations for 166 years (1805–1971). The primary disturbances resulting from cattle grazing are changes in vegetation, destabilization of eolian features, and increased sedimentation into Laguna Madre. The transition from grazing to non-grazing conditions has impacted the "beach" at Bird Island Basin, which now requires nourishment to be maintained.

- Wind energy. The mainland across from Padre Island National Seashore is the site of two wind power facilities with a total of 118 wind turbines that each generates 2.4 megawatts of electricity. The primary concerns regarding the development of wind energy in the vicinity of the national seashore are impacts on migrating bird and marine species, changes in fishing pressure (i.e., bait fish congregate near structures for food and shelter, thereby attracting predator species), changes in habitat as a result of transmission lines (i.e., alterations in magnetic field may affect sea turtle migration), and terrestrial impacts of routing a right-of-way across the national seashore to access the power grid.

The glossary contains explanations of many technical terms used in this report, including terms used in the Map Unit Properties Table. Refer to figure 14 for a geologic time scale.

Acknowledgements

The Geologic Resources Inventory (GRI) is one of 12 inventories funded by the National Park Service Inventory and Monitoring Program. The GRI is administered by the Geologic Resources Division of the Natural Resource Program Center.

The Geologic Resources Division relies heavily on partnerships with institutions such as the U.S. Geological Survey, Colorado State University, state geologic surveys, local museums, and universities in developing GRI products.

Special thanks to: Darrell Echols with whom the author had numerous phone conversations and e-mail communications regarding the geologic issues at Padre Island National Seashore. Darrell Echols served as park biologist at the national seashore from 1999 to 2003 and chief of resource management from 2003 to 2008. He currently serves as the deputy superintendent of the National Park Service, Outer Banks Group.

Edward Kassman and Pat O'Dell (NPS Geologic Resources Division) provided information regarding oil and gas operations and regulations.

Rebecca Beavers (NPS Geologic Resources Division) provided many of the photographs in the report.

Credits

Author
Katie KellerLynn (Colorado State University)

Review
Darrell Echols (NPS Outer Banks Group)
Jim Gibeaut (Texas A&M University-Corpus Christi)
Courtney Schupp (Assateague Island National Seashore)
Rebecca Beavers (NPS Geologic Resources Division)
Jason Kenworthy (NPS Geologic Resources Division)

Editing
Diane Lane

Digital Geologic Data Production
Ron Karpilo (Colorado State University)
Stephanie O'Meara (Colorado State University)

Digital Geologic Data Overview Layout Design
Georgia Hybels(NPS Geologic Resources Division)
David Green (Colorado State University)

Introduction

The following section briefly describes the National Park Service Geologic Resources Inventory and the regional geologic setting of Padre Island National Seashore.

Purpose of the Geologic Resources Inventory

The Geologic Resources Inventory (GRI) is one of 12 inventories funded by the National Park Service (NPS) Inventory and Monitoring Program. The GRI, administered by the Geologic Resources Division of the Natural Resource Program Center, is designed to provide and enhance baseline information available to park managers. The GRI team relies heavily on partnerships with institutions such as the U.S. Geological Survey, Colorado State University, state geologic surveys, local museums, and universities in developing GRI products.

The goals of the GRI are to increase understanding of the geologic processes at work in parks and to provide sound geologic information for use in park decision making. Sound park stewardship requires an understanding of the natural resources and their role in the ecosystem. Park ecosystems are fundamentally shaped by geology. The compilation and use of natural resource information by park managers is called for in section 204 of the National Parks Omnibus Management Act of 1998 and in NPS-75, Natural Resources Inventory and Monitoring Guideline.

To realize these goals, the GRI team is systematically conducting a scoping meeting for each of the 270 identified natural area parks and providing a park-specific digital geologic map and geologic report. These products support the stewardship of park resources and are designed for nongeoscientists. Scoping meetings bring together park staff and geologic experts to review available geologic maps and discuss specific geologic issues, features, and processes.

The GRI mapping team converts the geologic maps identified for park use at the scoping meeting into digital geologic data in accordance with their Geographic Information Systems (GIS) Data Model. These digital data sets bring an interactive dimension to traditional paper maps. The digital data sets provide geologic data for use in park GIS and facilitate the incorporation of geologic considerations into a wide range of resource management applications. The newest maps contain interactive help files. This geologic report assists park managers in the use of the map and provides an overview of park geology and geologic resource management issues.

For additional information regarding the content of this report and current GRI contact information please refer to the Geologic Resources Inventory web site (http://www.nature.nps.gov/geology/inventory/).

Park Setting

Padre Island National Seashore is relatively undeveloped because of its remote location, National Park System designation, and lack of permanent roads. The major population center in the vicinity of the national seashore is Corpus Christi to the north, in Nueces County (fig. 1). Port Mansfield is near the southern boundary of the seashore, across the Mansfield Channel in Willacy County, and the towns of Laguna Vista, Laguna Heights, Port Isabel, and South Padre Island are to the south of the national seashore in Cameron County. The lack of development on the mainland adjacent to the national seashore in Kleberg and Kenedy counties is largely a result of the conservation of 18,287 ha (45,187 ac) in the Laguna Atascosa Unit of Laguna Atascosa National Wildlife Refuge, as well as undeveloped state lands and large, privately owned ranches, such as the King and Kenedy.

Long, narrow Padre Island National Seashore covers 52,745 ha (130,332 ac) and separates Laguna Madre from the Gulf of Mexico. Of the national seashore's four sides, three are in water (fig. 1). The eastern boundary runs for 105 km (65 mi) in the Gulf of Mexico. The western boundary is located in Laguna Madre, the world's largest hypersaline estuary. Marking the southern boundary is Mansfield Channel, which cuts through the island and estuary to Port Mansfield, Texas. North Beach marks the terrestrial northern boundary.

The northern part of the national seashore is generally higher and wider than the southern part. The northern part consists of broad beaches; large, stabilized foredunes; grasslands; and large, shifting back-island dunes (table 1). The average depth of Laguna Madre in this area is about 1.2 m (4 ft). The Gulf Intracoastal Waterway—a segment of the Intracoastal Waterway that runs between New York and Brownsville, Texas—traverses the entire length of Laguna Madre and marks a part of the seashore's western boundary in the northern part of the national seashore. Dredged material from the waterway forms spoil banks varying from 0.4 to 2.0 ha (1 to 5 ac) in area. Two natural islands—North Bird and South Bird—are situated at the northern end of the national seashore within Laguna Madre. Both the islands and spoil mounds are significant bird rookeries.

South of Malaquite Visitor Center, the convergence of longshore currents from the north and south changes the island's character. Here, steeper topography and an abundance of shells are typical of the beaches whose names reflect the setting (i.e., Little Shell Beach and Big Shell Beach). High foredunes, grasslands, and extensive barrier flats also characterize this segment of shoreline.

In the southern half of the national seashore, south of Big Shell Beach, the beaches are flat, the foredunes are few, and the vegetation is sparse. After storms, temporary passes (washover channels) allow Laguna Madre to drain into the Gulf of Mexico. When these passes close, ponds that are left behind support fish for many months before drying up. These ponds also attract wintering birds.

Padre Island History

Throughout its history, Padre Island has been known by several names: "la Isla Blanca" (White Island), "Isla de los Malaguitas" (Island of the Malaquites, a band of the Karankawa people who were nomadic hunter-gatherers), and most recently, "Padre Island" (named for Padre Nicolas Ballí, a Spanish priest and the first permanent settler in 1804). Four nations have owned Padre Island. The first was Spain, which owned the island from its entry into the New World until the Mexican Revolution of 1820. Following the revolution, Mexico owned Padre Island from 1821 until 1836, when the newly formed Republic of Texas claimed the area between the Nueces River and the Rio Grande. Padre Island was under ownership by the Republic of Texas until its territory was acquired by the United States following the United States–Mexican War.

Padre Island's history has revolved around ranching. Padre Ballí introduced cattle to the island, and for three decades Ballí and his nephew Juan José used Padre Island for cattle grazing, which continued under various hands until 1971, when the National Park Service removed cattle from Padre Island National Seashore. At the end of the United States–Mexican War in 1848, Americans replaced Mexicans as the island's ranchers. By the time of the Civil War (1861–1865), the island supported a small community of cattle ranchers. In 1876, Patrick Dunn, an Irishman, moved to Padre Island and developed a large cattle ranch, and ultimately acquired nearly all of Padre Island. His family enterprise continued until 1971.

The most prominent and lasting exceptions to ranching as the sole enterprise on Padre Island have been the development of the tourism industry (including the development of the town of South Padre Island and the national seashore) beginning in the early 1920s, and the exploration and development of the island's oil and gas reserves, which began in the 1950s (National Park Service 2009).

The age of the automobile and the construction of a causeway brought tourism to the island (Callaway 1972). Col. Sam Robertson, an early South Texas developer who had dreams of establishing tourist facilities on the island, purchased the land from Patrick Dunn in 1926, although Dunn retained the mineral and grazing rights. Robertson opened the causeway to the public on July 4, 1927; the causeway ran from Flour Bluff, east of Corpus Christi, to Padre Island. Tourists expecting a leisurely drive were rudely awakened by timber with troughs set to accommodate the wheels of a Model T Ford; low guard rails provided little protection for a vehicle that might bounce out of its trough (Callaway 1972). The wooden supports of this causeway are still visible across the flats of Laguna Madre. Robertson also operated two ferry crossings—one at Port Aransas and the other at Port Isabel. Ultimately, the Great Depression broke Robertson, and his dreams of land investment, development, and tourism were never fully realized (Sheire 1971).

In the 1930s, plans for a state park on the island were proposed (National Park Service 1973), but World War II curtailed ideas of development. "The hopes of many enterprising businessmen lay dormant until 1950" (Callaway 1972, p. 30), when concern that the nation's shoreline would become entirely developed focused attention on Padre Island's outstanding natural features. In 1954 the National Park Service recommended establishment of three national seashores; one of these was Padre Island. The congressional approval necessary for the transfer of state lands and the acquisition of private lands took 9 years (Callaway 1972) but was achieved in 1962 with the passage of Public Law 87-712.

The limitation of $5 million in the original bill made it necessary to return to Congress for separate bills (Public Law 90-594 and 91-42) to authorize additional funds for acquisition. Padre Island National Seashore opened to the public in 1963.

Table 1. Land cover in Padre Island National Seashore

Classification type	Areal extent		Percentage of national seashore
	Hectares	Acres	
Beach/sand	1,319	3,259	2.5
Dunes (foredunes and back-island dunes)	2,480	6,127	4.7
Emergent vegetation	7,800	19,273	14.8
Grassland	5,434	13,427	10.3
Gulf of Mexico	5,170	12,775	9.8
Inland waters (ephemeral and permanent freshwater ponds)	949	2,346	1.8
Laguna Madre	12,345	30,503	23.4
Rookery islands	106	261	0.2
Sparse vegetation	2,459	6,075	4.6
Unconsolidated shore	2,638	6,518	5.0
Urban (developed areas)	158	391	0.3
Washover channels	482	1,192	0.9
Wind-tidal flats	11,448	28,287	21.7
Total	**52,788**	**130,434[1]**	**100.0**

1 Total acreage is 130,434; federal acreage is 130,355; nonfederal acreage is 79. Data from National Park Service (2000).

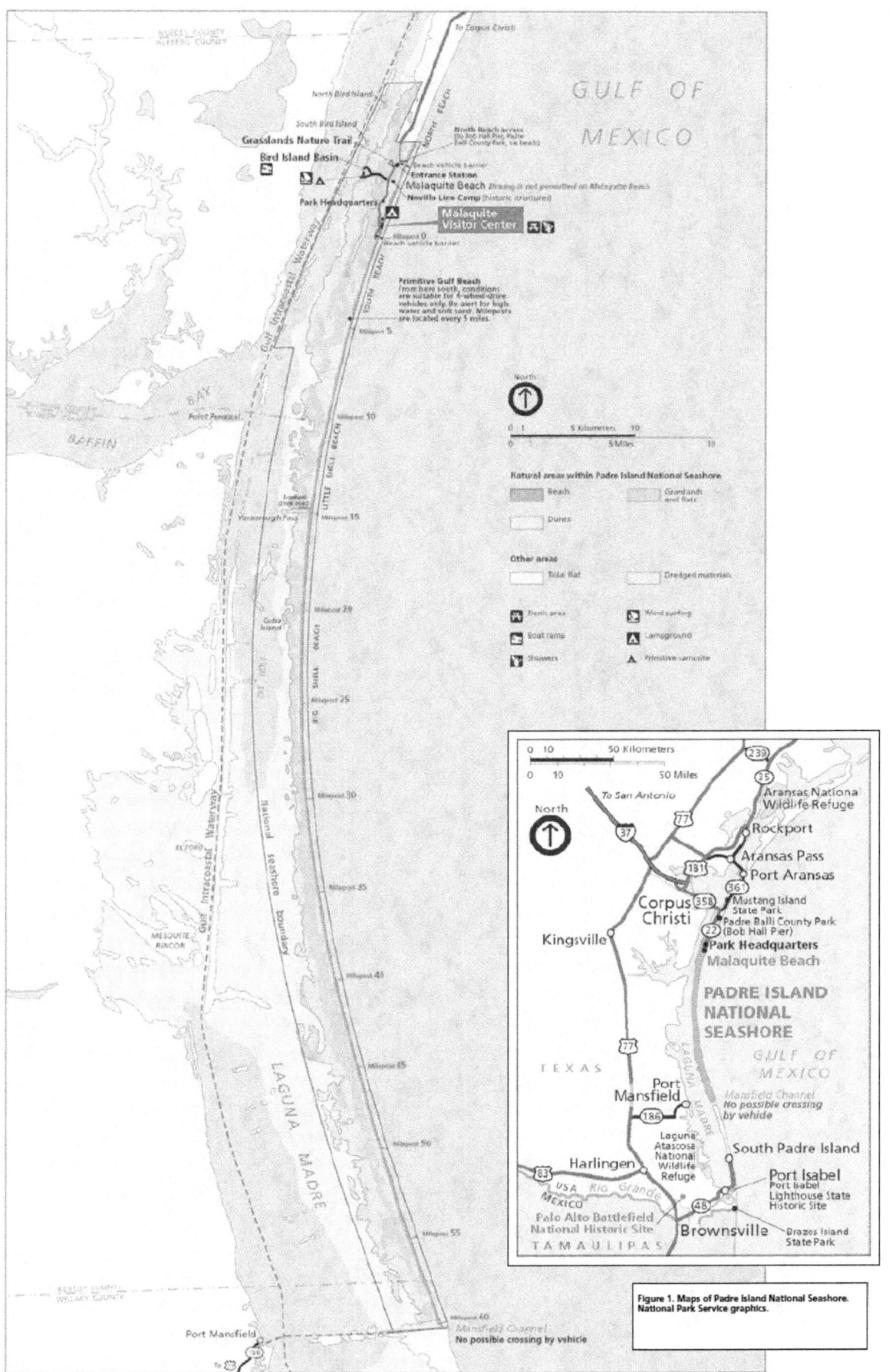

Figure 1. Maps of Padre Island National Seashore.
National Park Service graphics.

Geologic Issues

The Geologic Resources Division held a Geologic Resources Inventory scoping session for Padre Island National Seashore on May 12–14, 2003, to discuss geologic resources, address the status of geologic mapping, and assess resource management issues and needs. This section synthesizes the scoping results, in particular those issues that may require attention from resource managers. Contact the Geologic Resources Division for technical assistance.

During scoping, participants did not prioritize the geologic issues affecting resource management at Padre Island National Seashore. They are organized here into two main groups: natural issues (Coastal Vulerability, Blowing Sand and Dune Development, Hurricanes, Benthic Habitat Mapping, and Paleontological Resources) and anthropogenic issues (Bird Island Basin, Vehicle Impacts, Dredging, Oil and Gas Operations, Shoreline Debris, Grazing, and Wind Energy).

Coastal Vulnerability

On the basis of six variables—geomorphology, shoreline change (erosion/accretion), regional coastal slope, relative sea-level change, mean significant wave height, and mean tidal range—investigators determined the coastal vulnerability of Padre Island National Seashore to sea-level rise (fig. 2) (Pendleton et al. 2004). Sea-level rise projections vary widely depending on location, future emissions scenarios, and modeling technique. Globally, at least 0.18 m to 0.59 m (7 in. to 2 ft) of sea level rise is projected by 2100 (Meehl et al. 2007; National Park Service 2010a). Some projections summarized by Karl et al. (2009) suggest much larger increases in sea level. For example, Rahmstorf (2007) projected global sea levels to rise between 0.5 and 1.4 m (1.6 and 4.6 ft) above the 1990 level by 2100. For South Texas, a 37-year-long tide-gauge record shows that relative sea level has risen at a rate of 4.6 mm/yr (0.18 in/yr) at Rockport (since 1948), 2.05 mm/yr (0.08 in/yr) at Port Mansfield (since 1963), and 3.44 mm/yr (0.14 in/yr) at South Padre Island (since 1958) (Zervas 2001). This record inherently includes both worldwide changes in sea level (eustatic) and regional changes in sea level (isostatic and tectonic adjustments of the land surface). The relative rise in sea level at Port Isabel is the lowest for the entire Texas coast (Morton and Holmes 2009). The rate of relative sea-level rise in Laguna Madre is 3.4 mm/year (0.14 in/year), which is nearly comparable to the average global eustatic rate of 3.1 mm/year (0.12 in/year) between 1993 and 2003 (Parry et al. 2007).

Human activity, particularly through the emission of greenhouse gases, is very likely (more than 90% certain) contributing to global warming (IPCC 2007) and thus accelerating the rate of climate change and global sea level rise. Karl et al. (2009) summarized climate change impacts for the Southeast and coastal regions of the United States. Along with increases in air and ocean surface temperatures and sea-level rise, hurricane intensity is expected to increase. Maximum storm surges are also projected to increase. These impacts will be particularly acute on vulnerable barrier islands. For more information regarding climate change, effects throughout the National Park Service, and the NPS response, visit the NPS Climate Change Response Program website: http://www.nature.nps.gov/climatechange/index.cfm.

At Padre Island National Seashore, beach composition, dune height, and washover channels are key geomorphic features affecting coastal vulnerability. These features determine the relative resistance to erosion. For example, beaches having large dunes erode more slowly than beaches having low dunes or no dunes (Morton 2003). Furthermore, lithologic composition and hardness (e.g., loose sand vs. compacted shell) influence the erodibility of beaches (Morton 2003).

Investigators determined that 17% of the Gulf of Mexico shoreline at Padre Island National Seashore has very high vulnerability to future sea-level rise, 28% has high vulnerability, 29% has moderate vulnerability, and 26% has low vulnerability (Pendleton et al. 2004). Vulnerable sections of coastlines are more susceptible to shoreline erosion and land loss, saltwater intrusion into aquifers, inundation of wetlands and estuaries, loss of cultural and historic resources, and damage to infrastructure (Pendleton et al. 2004). In areas where beaches and wetlands migrate inland to survive elevated sea levels and increased storm surge, land managers must consider protection and retreat strategies for vulnerable coastal resources (Beavers 2005).

On the basis of morphology, investigators divided Padre Island National Seashore into three sections: northern, central, and southern (Pendleton et al. 2004). This tripartite division highlights the significance of the six coastal-vulnerability variables and facilitates discussion and planning. The area in the national seashore most vulnerable to future sea-level rise is the southernmost segment (fig. 2). This segment is a "low profile barrier" (Morton et al. 2004) consisting of sandy beaches and a discontinuous ridgeline of unstable dunes. Numerous overwash channels cut across the island in this segment of the seashore. With respect to geomorphology, the low dunes and washover channels influenced the ranking; this part of the seashore also has a history of high shoreline erosion.

The gently sloping, sandy Malaquite Beach serves as an example of the northern segment of shoreline. Although the dunes in this segment of the national seashore are relatively stable and continuous, they are of only moderate size. In addition, vehicular traffic suppresses dune formation and results in significant shoreline erosion. Hence, investigators ranked this part of Padre Island National Seashore as highly vulnerable to future sea-level rise.

Central Padre Island National Seashore has steep beaches consisting mostly of shells. Big Shell Beach exemplifies this central segment. Referred to as a "high profile barrier" by Morton et al. (2004), the central segment has nearly continuous foredunes as much as 15 m (50 ft) high, many of which are stabilized by vegetation. This segment of shoreline ranked either moderate (below latitude 27°N [approximately milepost 30]) or low (above latitude 27°N) in shoreline vulnerability because of its high dune ridgeline and history of shoreline accretion (see "Geologic History").

Rates of shoreline change in the various segments of the national seashore range from greater than 2 m (0.6 ft) of erosion per year to 2 m (0.6 ft) of accretion per year, with the greatest accretion occurring at the midpoint of Padre Island National Seashore.

Bush and Young (2009) have suggested 7 "vital signs" and methods for monitoring coastal features and processes: shoreline change; coastal dune morphology; coastal vegetation cover; topography/elevation; composition of beach material; wetland position/acreage, and coastal wetland accretion.

Blowing Sand and Dune Development
Blowing sand is ubiquitous at Padre Island National Seashore. Blowing sand can require many hours of maintenance. Since the national seashore's establishment, facility managers have employed a variety of techniques to mitigate blowing sand, for example, planting vegetation and then erecting fences and posting signs to protect the plants, posting signs to discourage traffic on existing vegetation, and spreading oyster shells over barren areas or covering them with hay made from native grasses (Weise and White 1980). Today, bulldozers continuously scrape windblown sand off the paved parking lot at Malaquite Beach. Tongues of sand blown by onshore winds creep relentlessly onto park roads (fig. 3). Eolian sand routinely engulfs the patrol cabin at milepost 42 (Darrell Echols, National Park Service, telephone communication, May 1, 2009).

Nevertheless, from a geomorphic perspective, and from many angles of a resource management perspective, blowing sand is a "good thing" in that blowing sand creates dunes, which protect the island and mainland from storm surge (see "Hurricanes"). The barrier island provides a buffer zone, absorbing the high wind and wave energies of tropical storms and thus lessening the impact on the mainland. If the fragile dunes of the barrier island are damaged by development, then the first line of coastal storm defense is weakened (Boylan 1986).

A major impact from development occurred in 1969 with the placement of the Malaquite facilities within the fore-island dune ridge. Contractors removed the foredunes to provide space for the buildings and create an ocean view for visitors. The Malaquite pavilion had continuous structural problems, and Hurricane Allen weakened it in 1980. Damage fully manifested itself several years after this hurricane, when park staff reported patches of falling concrete. Saltwater that had infiltrated the building during the storm had finally reached the steel supports and led to flaking concrete. By January 1986 the Malaquite Beach pavilion could no longer withstand daily use without being a safety hazard (Jones 1999).

At this same time, park planners began recognizing the necessity of "maintaining the island's defense" and designed new facilities at Malaquite Beach to conform to the island's natural processes, rather than trying to adjust them to fit human needs (Jones 1999). Opened in July 1989, the visitor center at Malaquite Beach was built behind the foredune ridge. However, part of the landing and the boardwalk were situated within the "nonexistent" foredune ridgeline. As the ridgeline has begun to reestablish itself, blowing sand continually covers the boardwalk, which leads to the beach. Park employees have added sand fencing and vegetation to help direct sand away from the structure and stabilize the dune, but sand continues to fill in around the boardwalk and up towards the landing. As stated in a 2001 NPS memo, "the dune line is functioning normally so we can expect the sand to continue to cover the walkway as long as the dune is unvegetated" (Ken McMullen, Padre Island National Seashore, memorandum, May 2001).

Short-term solutions to protect the existing walkway at the Malaquite Visitor Center include (1) raising the height of the existing sand fences to screen more sand, (2) vegetating the dune to stabilize blowing sand, and (3) extending the sand fence approximately 9 m (30 ft) to reduce the amount of sand that is blown around the walkway (Ken McMullen, Padre Island National Seashore, memorandum, May 2001). For similar situations, Conti (2007) proposed vertical barriers made of plywood, silt fencing, or geotextiles attached to the handrails of elevated walkways as temporary solutions. Other simple solutions, though time consuming, are shoveling sand off the structure or simply continuing to walk over the deposited sand.

The long-term solution is to relocate the present walkway (Ken McMullen, Padre Island National Seashore, memorandum, May 2001). Conti (2007) suggests the following construction methods, which may be applicable to Padre Island:

- Construct walkway, including terminus, above the surface of the surrounding dunes.
- Construct walkway with at least a 1:1 height-to-width ratio. This promotes growth of vegetation by reducing shading.
- Space deck boards at least 1.3 cm (0.5 in) between adjacent boards to allow rain, sunlight, and deposited sand to reach the underlying surface.
- Orient the walkway terminus away (leeward) from the prevailing wind to reduce sand accumulation.

- Construct walkway away from sources of loose, unstable sand such as piles resulting from beach maintenance.

Hurricanes

Padre Island has had a history of hurricane events (table 2). In the Gulf of Mexico, a major hurricane causes land losses and substantial property damage about every 10 years (Hayes 1967; Nummedal et al. 1980; Morton and Paine 1985). Making landfall at Port Lavaca, Hurricane Carla in 1961 is remembered for its storm surge. In 1967, Hurricane Beulah spawned torrential rainfall and more than 100 tornadoes. Hurricane Celia in 1970 was characterized by extreme wind velocities (Brown et al. 1976, 1977, 1980). Hurricane Allen, one of the greatest hurricanes of the 20th century, stalled and lost strength as it approached the Texas coast in August 1980. However, the hurricane's impact was severe along the national seashore, where storm surge heights were approximately 3 m (10 ft) above mean sea level. The myriad effects of Hurricane Allen on Padre Island closely followed the pattern of previous hurricanes (Weise and White 1980). Hurricane Allen reoccupied more than 60 washover channels, destroying segments of the main road that runs the length of South Padre Island (Morton et al. 2004).

Recent storm events include Hurricane Dolly (July 23, 2008). This storm made landfall on Padre Island and caused extensive damage to the town of South Padre Island. In July 2010, the island received heavy rains from Hurricane Alex, but the storm left the island generally unscathed (Barajas 2010). The most-recent, major hurricane to hit Padre Island National Seashore was Hurricane Bret in August 1999. Originating off the coast of Nicaragua, Hurricane Bret peaked in intensity as a category 4 storm (on the Saffir-Simpson hurricane intensity scale). As it made its turn towards Texas, the storm began encountering much cooler sea-surface temperatures near the coast; the weakening system made landfall in sparsely populated Kenedy County, striking the national seashore in the area from milepost 32.5 south to the milepost 56.8 (National Park Service 2000) (see fig. 1). Winds reached 225 km/h (140 mph). The hurricane also produced six coastal tornadoes inland as far as Burnet County (Roth 2004). The storm surge cut 12 washover channels into Padre Island; three were major.

Most hurricanes hitting the Texas coast originate in the Caribbean Sea or Gulf of Mexico (Weise and White 1980). Hurricanes entering or originating in the Gulf of Mexico normally follow a northward or westward path. Because a hurricane spirals in a counterclockwise direction in the Northern Hemisphere, it develops a larger storm surge on its right side as it approaches the coastline. As such, flooding will be greater in low-lying areas to the right of the hurricane as viewed from the approaching eye of the storm (Weise and White 1980).

As a hurricane approaches mainland Texas along the central Gulf of Mexico coast, barrier islands are the first land feature in the path of the surge. Where a well-developed, fore-island dune ridge exists (e.g., along Big

Shell Beach), a barrier island provides a line of defense for the back-island and mainland; the barrier helps to block the surge and dissipate large amounts of wave and current energy (Weise and White 1980). However, storm surge produced by hurricanes does not always stop at the beach and fore-island area. If a category 2 or stronger hurricane makes landfall near Padre Island National Seashore, storm surge will likely inundate the cuts between the dunes. If water levels rise sufficiently high to allow wave attack, dune erosion could be severe (U.S. Geological Survey 2008). Furthermore, the surge may wash across low-lying segments of barrier islands, breaching the fore-island dune ridge and scouring washover channels (Scott et al. 1969) (see "Storm Washover Channels and Fans"). Hurricane intensity and associated storm surges are projected to increase as climate continues to warm (Karl et al. 2009).

In geologic terms, hurricanes accelerate coastal processes so that during the hours of storm passage, the degree of erosion and deposition in coastal systems amounts to what would normally take months or even years (Price 1958; Hayes 1967; McGowen et al. 1970; McGowen and Scott 1975; Brown et al. 1976, 1977, 1980; McGowen et al. 1977; Morton and McGowen 1980).

Hurricanes produce a gently sloping, nearly planar hurricane beach (Hayes 1965). When the hurricane has passed, normal processes resume and, in time, a normal beach profile is restored. Sand eroded from the beach during the hurricane is gradually carried back by fair–weather wave action to rebuild the normal backshore and foreshore. A lowered backshore may persist for several years between hurricanes because it is outside the influence of normal wave actions (Hill and Hunter 1987). Longshore drift smoothes irregularities in the Gulf of Mexico shoreline and builds bars and beaches across the mouths of the hurricane channels (Weise and White 1980).

Benthic Habitat Mapping

Padre Island National Seashore contains 42 km² (16 mi²) of marine resources. That is, the national seashore's eastern boundary extends approximately 0.4 km (0.25 mi) into the Gulf of Mexico. The characteristics of this offshore region are only generally known, however, because mapping has not been completed. Mapping of the area would clarify the land-water interface; marine relationships to terrestrial features; bathymetric features, such as navigation hazards; seafloor features that influence waves, currents, and storm surge; the areal extent and health of marine resources, including seafloor habitat and species; sediment characterization and quality as habitat; and the location and assessment of shipwrecks, anthropogenic debris, and marine archaeological artifacts and sites.

To date, two investigators have compiled preliminary data for use in a future benthic habitat map for Padre Island National Seashore. In 2001, Dr. Jennifer Rahn from Baylor University, an NPS Geoscientist-in-the-Park, completed an assessment of GIS data covering coastal processes and geomorphology along Padre Island

National Seashore, with particular emphasis on the effects of U.S. Army Corps of Engineers projects (Lisa Norby, Geologic Resources Division, e-mail message, August 24, 2009). These data are retained in the Natural Resources Division office at Padre Island National Seashore. In addition, GeoCorps America researcher Lisa Fay completed an assessment of existing geospatial data for Padre Island National Seashore in June 2008. These data are retained in Geologic Resources Division files in Lakewood, Colorado.

The National Park Service has collaborated with partners to produce detailed benthic-habitat classification maps for some of the marine areas within and adjacent to National Park System units. This is a multidisciplinary task that combines geological, biological, oceanographic, and chemical components. The intent of such projects is to facilitate the management, interpretation, and understanding of park resources by providing baseline maps, a GIS database, and descriptions of the biological and geological resources of marine lands (Gibbs et al. 2007). In 2007 the U.S. Geological Survey collaborated with the National Park Service to create benthic-habitat classification maps for Puʻukoholā Heiau National Historic Site and Kaloko-Honokōhau National Historical Park in Hawaiʻi, using existing color aerial photography, scanning hydrographic operational airborne LIDAR (light detection and ranging) survey (SHOALS), georeferenced underwater video, and still photography (Cochran et al. 2007; Gibbs et al. 2007). Collaborators within the National Park Service for such a project for Padre Island National Seashore would include staff from the national seashore, Geologic Resources Division, Gulf Coast Network, and Ocean and Coastal Resources Branch of the Water Resources Division.

Paleontological Resources

Investigators have not conducted any formal field-based paleontological resource surveys for Padre Island National Seashore (Kenworthy et al. 2007). However, the national seashore's museum collection contains 13 paleontological specimens that either park staff or visitors found within the national seashore; most specimens had washed ashore (Kenworthy et al. 2007). Museum specimens include bone fragments of mammalian limbs, a mammalian acetabulum (pelvis), lower molars of a bison and horse, mammoth teeth or tooth plates, possible remains of a giant tortoise, and a number of unidentifiable bone fragments. The age of the specimens ranges from Pleistocene (2.6 million to 11,700 years ago) to Holocene (11,700 years ago to present) (Kenworthy et al. 2007).

While the island itself is not a major source of paleontological resources, fossils from the offshore Pleistocene Seven and One-Half Fathom Reef have washed ashore. Although this reef is submerged outside the national seashore's boundaries, it is likely the source of most of the seashore's paleontological resources. The reef—interpreted by Thayer et al. (1974) as a late Pleistocene intermittent lake deposit—is approximately 50 m (164 ft) wide and 350 m (1,148 ft) long, having a

maximum relief of 5.4 m (18 ft). It is located 3.2 km (2 mi) offshore, 74 km (46 mi) south of the national seashore's northern entrance in approximately 14 m (46 ft) of water (Thayer et al. 1974). These lake sediments were submerged as sea level rose during the Holocene Epoch. As a result of their relative hardness (well-cemented sandy marl), they now form an underwater ridge.

In addition, Lundelius (1972) described the Pleistocene Ingleside fauna from a fossil locality near Corpus Christi. This locality is one of the largest and most diverse known in Texas and contains 42 vertebrate taxa, including mammals, birds, reptiles, amphibians, and fish (Lundelius 1972). Although this deposit does not occur within Padre Island National Seashore, these fauna illustrate the diversity of paleontological resources in the vicinity of the national seashore. McBride and Honda (1994) described exposures of the Ingleside Barrier Complex along the western margin of Laguna Madre, 8 km (13 mi) south of Baffin Bay. These exposures—beach sandstone contemporaneous with the Ingleside fauna—contain fossils in the form of a shell coquina.

Miller and Hunter (1979) recovered Pleistocene shells from subsurface lagoonal deposits within Padre Island National Seashore. Radiocarbon dates of dwarf surf clam (*Mulinia lateralis*) from two wells—approximately 21 m (69 ft) below sea level—ranged in age from 29,980 to 27,380 years before present (Miller and Hunter 1979). The deposit contains a fossil shell layer 8–15 m (26–49 ft) below modern sea level in the southern part of Padre Island and about 19 m (62 ft) below modern sea level in the northern reaches. This subsurface layer hosts more than 90 species of marine invertebrates and one terrestrial snail.

Spoil mounds associated with dredging of local channels may also host Pleistocene fossils, coquina, or serpulid (worm) reef material. Although obviously not in situ, the piles provide an opportunity to view the subsurface sediments and paleontological resources of Padre Island National Seashore's Laguna Madre (Kenworthy et al. 2007).

Continued discovery of fossils on the shoreline of Padre Island is very probable (Kenworthy et al. 2007). Although modern, unoccupied shells can be collected within Padre Island National Seashore, collecting paleontological resources of any type is not permissible. This dichotomy can cause some confusion among the visiting public. Hence, Kenworthy et al. (2007) recommended continued interpretation and education because distinguishing between modern and fossil shells can be difficult. Shell collecting may bring newly discovered paleontological specimens to light, and education may decrease illegal (though typically unintentional) collecting. In addition, Kenworthy et al. (2007) recommended continuing to maintain the museum collection, increasing staff awareness of material that may wash ashore, retaining potentially identifiable material to be included in the collection, and consulting local experts for identification.

The 2009 Paleontological Resources Preservation Act directs the Secretaries of Interior and Agriculture to implement comprehensive, science-based resource management programs for fossils, which are non-renewable. The NPS and other federal land managing agencies are developing joint regulations associated with the Act.

Bird Island Basin

In 2000, 71,700 people visited Bird Island Basin (Withers et al. 2004) because of its "fantastic opportunities for windsurfing, kayaking, boating, and fishing" (National Park Service 2010b). Additionally, camping sites, both recreational vehicle and tent, are available in the area.

Human use has modified the landscape and affected the geologic processes operating at Bird Island Basin. Processes requiring management attention are shoreline erosion, infilling and sedimentation of the boat basin, erosion via runoff, and reduction in sand supply. Withers et al. (2004) suggested alternatives to mitigate adverse effects on geologic processes while accommodating a variety of recreational activities. Since 2004, park managers have ameliorated many of the geologic and visitor-use problems by upgrading the infrastructure at Bird Island Basin. However, two issues still require attention: restoring the shoreline adjacent to the boat ramp and fully opening the overwash area from the channel into the mudflat west of Bird Island Basin (Darrell Echols, National Park Service, e-mail message, July 6, 2009).

Shoreline Erosion

Investigators have attributed some shoreline erosion to vehicular traffic and parking on the shore, at least locally (National Park Service 1995; Withers et al. 2004; Smith-Engle et al. 2006). The area is being compressed by the weight of the vehicles and eroded away by the wave action in the lagoon (National Park Service 1994).

Sedimentation

The boat basin, which did not exist before 1964, is an artificial depression created via dredging. An isolated island just south of the basin and a small mound situated along the boat channel slightly west of the isolated island were built up by the dredged material. By 1969 a wind-tidal flat had prograded sufficiently as a result of increased eolian transport from drought and grazing to tie the small spoil mound to Padre Island; it remains connected today (Smith-Engle et al. 2006).

Runoff

During storms, runoff from the elevated road causes erosion (i.e., gullying). Investigators suggested using either some kind of reinforcement, such as a geotube, along the slope edge or physically adjusting the slope to direct most runoff back toward the wetland landward of the road (Smith-Engle et al. 2006).

Altered hydrologic conditions between Laguna Madre and the wind-tidal flat behind the shoreline require geologic engineering solutions. Creation of a raised beach profile west of the road would likely block the exchange of water, unless low points are incorporated at selected locations (Joel Wagner, Water Resources Division, written comment on Smith-Engle et al. 2006, June 5, 2006).

Beach Renourishment

Reduction in sand supply (and corresponding elimination of the beach) is a byproduct of the natural recovery of the island from overgrazing (see "Grazing"). The beach is an artifact of prior land use and is not viable without artificial maintenance (Rebecca Beavers, Geologic Resources Division, written comment on Smith-Engle et al. 2006, June 5, 2006). NPS management policies provide justification to renourish the beach at Bird Island Basin with the purpose of maintaining an altered shoreline in order to protect present development in the short run and focus high-density visitor use there, thus minimizing visitor impacts elsewhere in the short run. See section 4.8.1.1 of *Management Policies 2006* (National Park Service 2006a). Over the long term, it may be advisable for the park to seek a waiver of the NPS policy to allow shoreline processes to continue without interference. Factors supporting a waiver request include "the park's enabling statute which mentions 'public recreation' in the first sentence, the size of this shoreline at the time of the park's establishment, the high level of public use at this area, consistency with park planning documents and objectives, and the park's overall commitment to protection of natural processes" (Julia Brunner, Geologic Resources Division, written comment on Smith-Engle et al. 2006, June 5, 2006).

Four geologic factors would require consideration before renourishment commenced: (1) sediment (sand) size, (2) volume of sediment needed, (3) source of sediment, and (4) location/placement of sediment (Smith-Engle et al. 2006, 2007). Using fine-grained sand would mimic the existing geomorphic environment and provide the substrate to which users are accustomed. Using medium-grained sand would require less volume to achieve the same lifespan (table 3); however, the source of medium-grained sand is not local, so cost of materials and transport is a factor. In addition, medium-grained sand is "nonnative," with the potential for introducing invasive species in the imported sand (Courtney Schupp, National Park Service, written communication, September 30, 2009).

According to Smith-Engle et al. (2006), the optimal placement of sand is between the peninsula to the north, which was created by dredge material from the boat basin, and the entrance road to the south in the area of heaviest visitor use.

Vehicle Impacts

At the end of World War II, Patrick Dunn (see "History") purchased an army surplus truck, which he converted to a "bobtail" (Sheire 1971). This short, straight, four-wheel-drive (4WD) vehicle could move easily across the beaches of Padre Island. It changed the style of the cattle roundup, cutting the time necessary to gather the herd for market and reducing weight loss of the cattle by eliminating the month-long cattle drive up the island.

After 1971, cattle left the island, but 4WD vehicles used for other purposes stayed. The national seashore came into existence when personal ownership of 4WD vehicles was not widespread and exploring the beach in a "dune buggy" was considered a unique experience and rare treat (National Park Service 1973). Driving on beaches has become a common occurrence, and 101 km (63 mi) of the national seashore's beaches are open to vehicle traffic (fig. 4). Only 7.2 km (4.5 mi) of beach are off limits to vehicular traffic (i.e., the area between the North Beach and South Beach access roads, including Malaquite Beach). Beaches in the park are subject to Texas highway laws and regulations. All vehicles must be street legal and licensed. A high priority data need for Padre Island National Seashore is information about impacts of beach driving on park resources (Darrell Echols, Padre Island National Seashore, GRD technical assistance update, March 30, 2007).

Primarily in the 1970s and 1980s, various studies at Padre Island investigated this issue and found that beach driving

- Inhibits shoreline accretion and decreases the island's overall width (Behrens et al. 1976; Weise and White 1980).

- Increases shoreline erosion and instability during storms (Baccus and Horton 1979; Weise and White 1980).

- Eliminates the natural rebuilding capacity of the foredune system between storms (Behrens et al. 1975).

- Changes dune forms, creating plateaulike foredunes and lower elevations (McAtee 1975; McAtee and Drawe 1980).

- Inhibits formation of "embryo dunes" (coppice dunes) in front of the foredune ridge, tending to make the beach zone wider (McAtee 1975; McAtee and Drawe 1980).

- Creates blowouts by destroying vegetation that stabilizes dunes (Baccus and Horton 1979; Blum and Jones 1985).

- Reduces vegetation height, percentage cover, and the number of plant species present (McAtee 1975; McAtee and Drawe 1980).

- Changes species density and richness of vegetation and promotes the invasion of exotic species (Behrens et al. 1976; Baccus and Horton 1982; Lonard et al. 1999).

- Affects fauna (Baccus et al. 1977), including the endangered Kemp's ridley turtle (*Lepidochelys kempii*) (Echols and Kassman 2004).

- Changes the distribution of invertebrates such as ghost crabs (*Ocypode quadrata*) (Teerling 1970).

- Impacts benthic invertebrates and their habitat (Wicksten et al. 1987), which are an important food source for endangered piping plover (*Charadrius melodus*) (Dansby et al. 2008).

- Changes microenvironmental parameters (McAtee and Drawe 1981). As the intensity of human activity increased, elevation, especially of areas near the beach, decreased. Near the ground surface, average wind velocities, evaporation, atmospheric salinity, and wind-carried sand particles increased, as did soil salinity, soil pH, average soil temperature and range in temperature, soil bulk density, and soil moisture (with increasing depth) (McAtee and Drawe 1981).

The primary geomorphic processes affected by vehicular (and pedestrian) traffic are wind erosion, transport, and deposition. The mean annual wind speed at Padre Island National Seashore is 19 km/h (12 mph) (Hill and Hunter 1976). Where exposed beaches are crossed by winds that exceed 14 km/h (9 mph), sand is moved off the beach (Godfrey 1976). Wind velocities decrease near the ground surface, so sand lifted into the air is exposed to greater wind action. Vehicle wheels and foot traffic lift sand above the surface, exposing it to greater wind velocities and carrying it greater distances than under normal wind stress (Baccus and Horton 1982). Vegetation helps baffle the wind higher above the ground surface, entrapping more sand. However, vehicles and foot traffic crush and dislodge beach vegetation, destroying this capacity of plants to capture sand. As a result, areas with vehicular traffic have much smoother, flatter, and broader backbeach areas than those without vehicular traffic (Weise and White 1980). Such grading of beaches is detrimental to embryo (coppice) dune formation, as well as to pioneering and colonizing plant species (Baccus and Horton 1982).

Park managers began to anticipate the need to restrict access of 4WD vehicles to beaches and roads, prohibiting driving cross-country and over dunes. The 1973 master plan for the national seashore states, "Vehicle traffic may build to such an extent in the future that management will prohibit vehicles completely or permit them only on a reservation basis" (National Park Service 1973, p. 19) Padre Island National Seashore does not yet have a management plan for this popular activity. However, managers have established regulations that allow driving along the beach and within designated 4WD routes (i.e., Yarborough Pass and adjacent to Mansfield Channel) (Darrell Echols, National Park Service, e-mail message, July 6, 2009).

Considerations in the development of a management plan include the sensitivity of various environments; that is, some zones may be totally off limits, while others allow for increasing amounts of pedestrian or vehicular traffic. The digital geologic map may be useful in identifying these areas (see "Map Unit Properties Table"). For instance, damage to wind-tidal flats (i.e., map units L1, L2, and L3) may be irreparable. Tire tracks and footprints left more than 20 years ago are still present in some parts of wind-tidal flats (National Park Service 2006b). Sensitive areas also include marshes (units B4a, B4b, B4c, and B4d), foredunes (unit B3), coppice dunes (unit B2), other active dunes (unit B10), stabilized dunes (unit B5a), and vegetated barrier flats (unit B4) (Drawe and Ortega 1996; Withers 1996).

Although past studies have demonstrated the detrimental effects of vehicular traffic on the geomorphic, biologic, and microclimatologic processes and features in the national seashore (see above), park employees have identified specific questions about vehicular impacts that need scientific answers (Darrell Echols, Padre Island National Seashore, GRD technical assistance update, March 30, 2007):

- At what level of activity (i.e., number of vehicles) does ecological decline begin?

- What specific factors affect decline (e.g., vehicle weight or the number of passes within the same area)?

- What is the effect of tire ruts (puddles and channels) on the susceptibility of the system to erosion?

Managers want to ensure that any decisions regulating vehicle use are legally defensible and based on scientific data.

Dredging

Dredging is excavating in coastal environments, generally at least partly underwater. The process creates channels that make shallow waterways navigable or cuts passes through islands to connect water bodies. Dredging creates spoils (excess material), which are either disposed of in open water to the side of the channel or conveyed to a location away from the dredged area, for example, to a beach for renourishment. The environs of Padre Island National Seashore have been subject to dredging in many places.

Gulf Intracoastal Waterway

The Gulf Intracoastal Waterway, an artificial channel, extends the length of Laguna Madre, connecting Corpus Christi, Port Mansfield, Port Isabel, Port of Harlingen, and Brownsville. The waterway is 3.6 m (12 ft) deep and 38 m (125 ft) wide, cutting through the 209-km-(130-mi-) long lagoon. The U.S. Army Corps of Engineers constructed the channel in 1949 and maintains it through periodic dredging. Construction of the channel through the wind-tidal flats altered hydrodynamics by reducing both the frequency and duration of flooding (Rusnak 1960). Before dredging, strong or persistent winds from either the south or north would force water onto the flats, where it would remain until either gradually draining back into the permanently flooded part of Laguna Madre or evaporating. However, since its construction, the Gulf Intracoastal Waterway has provided an alternate route for the wind-driven water, and some water flows through the dredged channel rather than onto the flats (Breuer 1957; Rusnak 1960). Moreover, water that is driven onto the flats probably remains a shorter time because it can drain into the waterway rather than having to flow back across the flats (Courtney Schupp, National Park Service, written communication, September 29, 2009).

In addition, oil and gas operators dredged several shallow channels across Laguna Madre from the Gulf Intracoastal Waterway to access hydrocarbon well sites on the wind-tidal flats. Although these channels are not currently maintained by the operators, they are still present on the landscape. These channels are conduits for water flowing onto or off the flats. Field evidence indicates that the channels act primarily as drains: water draining off the flats erodes branching channels at the heads of the channels and locally lowers elevations of the surrounding flats (Morton and Holmes 2009).

As a result of the original construction and periodic maintenance of the Gulf Intracoastal Waterway, the U.S. Army Corps of Engineers has repeatedly disposed of dredge material (i.e., silt mixed with mud) in the open waters of Laguna Madre. Over the years, the dredge spoils have created banks stretching the length of the waterway. When surveyed in the 1970s, 109 spoil islands lined the waterway; an additional 40 were located along privately owned channels (Chaney et al. 1978). Currently, the U.S. Army Corps of Engineers uses 61 "placement areas" (i.e., spoil islands) along the main channel (U.S. Army Corps of Engineers 2003). Multiple islands make up each placement area, ranging from one to four islands (Darrell Echols, National Park Service, e-mail message, July 6, 2009). Ten of these placement areas are within the boundaries of Padre Island National Seashore (Darrell Echols, National Park Service, e-mail message, December 31, 2003). The spoil mounds (see "Map Unit Properties Table," units M1, M2, and M3) have become habitat for 25 species of colonial nesting waterbirds, including American white pelican (*Pelecanus onocrotalus*), great blue heron (*Ardea herodias*), reddish egret (*Egretta rufescens*), interior least tern (*Sterna antillarum athalassos*), sooty terns (*Onychoprion fuscatus*), and laughing gulls (*Leucophaeus atricilla*).

In the 1990s, the effects of dredging within Laguna Madre became a concern for conservation groups and sport-fishing enthusiasts (e.g., National Audubon Society and the Lower Laguna Madre Foundation) in the region. The groups' primary concern was that maintenance dredging in such a shallow lagoon was destroying seagrass beds, which are critical to the lagoon's waterbird habitat, fisheries, and overall biological productivity. The National Park Service was concerned about the effects of turbidity and contaminants from the dredge sediments.

In 1994, the National Audubon Society and its partners filed suit against the U.S. Army Corps of Engineers. The court ordered preparation of an environmental impact statement (EIS) and that all maintenance dredging stop (save for emergency dredging) in the interim. In response, the U.S. Army Corps of Engineers formed an interagency coordinating team (ICT) to review the effects of dredge disposal on Laguna Madre. Between 1993 and 2003, researchers completed 35 studies as part of the Laguna Madre Project, including the effects of dredge deposits on seagrass beds, wind-wave resuspension and circulation of sediment and dredge material, the effects of dredge material on piping (*Charadrius melodus*) and snowy (*C. alexandrinus*) plovers, temporal and spatial effects of the disposing of dredge material in open water on habitat of fishery and forage organisms, sediment budget analysis, benthic macroinfaunal analysis of areas where dredged material is placed, analysis of water and sediment quality, and tissue chemistry analysis (U.S. Army Corps of Engineers 2005).

The U.S. Army Corps of Engineers, along with the National Marine Fisheries Service, U.S. Fish and Wildlife Service (serving as the lead for the U.S. Department of the Interior), U.S. Environmental Protection Agency, Texas Parks and Wildlife Department, Texas General Land Office, Texas Water Development Board, Texas Department of Transportation, and Texas Natural Resource Conservation Commission (now the Texas Commission on Environmental Quality), formed the interagency coordinating team. The U.S. Coast Guard, National Park Service (Padre Island National Seashore), and Coastal Bend Bays and Estuaries Program served in secondary, advisory roles.

The ICT process resulted in the release of a final EIS (i.e., a 50-year dredge disposal plan). Some felt that more creative solutions could have resulted from the process (Texas Center for Policy Studies 2001). Nevertheless, the final EIS did address some of the National Park Service's concerns. The plan included the use of training levees to contain the dredge material for a short period of time. Once the sediment had settled out, the levees would be removed. This would help nesting shorebirds continue to use the islands because they could see the water and be aware of predators if the levees were removed (Darrell Echols, National Park Service, e-mail message, July 6, 2009). However, the National Park Service remained concerned that the dredging intervals suggested in the plan could impact seagrass beds in areas of open disposal; some research based on the estimated timelines for revegetation indicated that seagrass beds could be impaired. The U.S. Army Corps of Engineers addressed these concerns by stating that it would monitor the beds after disposal (Darrell Echols, National Park Service, e-mail message, July 6, 2009).

Mansfield Channel

Two artificial passes, Mansfield Channel and Brazos Santiago Pass, connect Laguna Madre to the Gulf of Mexico. Brazos Santiago Pass is south of Padre Island National Seashore in Cameron County. Mansfield Channel cuts through Padre Island and marks the southern extent of Padre Island National Seashore (fig. 1). The channel provides access to the Gulf Intracoastal Waterway and the fishing village at Port Mansfield. In September 1957 the Willacy County Navigation District completed the channel, but storms destroyed the pass and associated jetties in November of that same year. The U.S. Army Corps of Engineers completed the present channel and jetties in 1962 (Leatherwood 2008). Most recently, the Corps dredged the Mansfield Channel in April 2009. The dredge material was used to renourish beaches eroded during Hurricanes Dolly and Ike (2008) on the north side of the channel at the southernmost point of Padre Island National Seashore (Christensen 2009).

Besides facilitating boating access between Laguna Madre and the Gulf of Mexico, a long-standing justification for connecting the lagoon with the Gulf of

Mexico has been to reduce or moderate high salinities in the lagoon, an action thought to nurture more abundant fish and shrimp populations, such as redfish/red drum (*Sciaenops ocellatus*), brown shrimp (*Farfantepenaeus aztecus*), flounder (*Paralichthys lethostigma* and *P. abligutta*), and speckled trout/spotted seatrout (*Centropomus nebluosus*), thereby enhancing the sport and commercial fishing economy of Port Mansfield (Leatherwood 2008). However, given high rates of longshore drift of sediments, blowing sand, low tidal range, and no freshwater inflow, dredging the channel is a continuous process with high maintenance costs (Tunnell et al. 2002). Along the coast of Texas, generally only one natural pass per lagoon or bay system can be maintained by natural processes. Additional passes (i.e., artificial channels) reduce the tidal exchange through existing ones, necessitating increased dredging to maintain them (Brown et al. 1976, 1977, 1980). In addition, artificial channels alter the natural circulation pattern, allow greater tidal exchange between the Gulf of Mexico and Laguna Madre, and subject protected lagoonal waters to greater effects from storm surges (Morton 1994; Tunnell et al. 2002).

Yarborough Pass

Yarborough Pass, at milepost 15 between Little Shell and Big Shell beaches, is an example of a failed channel dredged repeatedly through Padre Island. In 1941, the Texas Game and Fish Commission excavated this channel in an attempt to provide an exchange between the Gulf of Mexico and Laguna Madre to reduce the high salinities in the lagoon's north-central section. The channel remained open for five months (Breuer 1957). Other unsuccessful attempts to create a channel were made in 1942, 1944, and finally 1952. Today, Yarborough is often flooded and filled with exceptionally deep and soft sand. It serves as one of two four-wheel-drive (4WD) areas running perpendicular to the island; the other is along Mansfield Channel.

Oil and Gas Operations

On March 23, 1951, Sun Oil Company (now Sunoco), headquartered in Philadelphia, Pennsylvania, drilled the first gas well within the current boundaries of Padre Island National Seashore. Since then other companies have explored for, and produced oil and gas from, the hydrocarbon reservoirs beneath Padre Island (fig. 5). The source rocks are the Oligocene (33 million to 28 million years old) Vicksburg and Frio formations (deltaic sandstone) and the lower and middle Miocene (23 million to 11 million years old) Fleming Formation (coastal-plain and continental-shelf clay and sandstone). In 1999, the U.S. Geological Survey estimated the total mean amount of undiscovered oil and gas within Padre Island National Seashore to be 52.67 million m^3 (65.74 billion ft^3) of gas and 40,776 m^3 (1.44 million ft^3) of natural gas liquids (Norby 2008).

Oil and gas operations are potential threats to park resources through accidental leaks and spills of hydrocarbons from pipelines and producing wells, groundwater contamination resulting from the injection of produced water into deep formations, and external oil spills (Withers et al. 2004).

Authorized operators must follow regulations in 36 Code of Federal Regulations (CFR), Part 9, Subpart B ("9B regulations"), which require each oil and gas operator to develop a plan of operation that outlines the specific location, process, and protection measures that it will employ. The National Park Service evaluates the submitted plan and determines whether operations will affect park visitors or resources and, if so, how to eliminate, minimize, or mitigate impacts.

Park policy requires that operators use best available technology. The National Park Service reviews and updates established mitigation measures, evaluates past practices, applies current research findings, incorporates public comment, and coordinates with partners to preserve and protect park resources. These actions help provide an enjoyable visitor experience and protect park natural and cultural resources while allowing congressionally mandated access to nonfederal oil and gas resources (National Park Service 2006d).

The National Park Service has developed many mitigation measures to minimize or eliminate the impacts on park resources and visitor experiences. Mitigation measures include the following:

- Limiting the maximum speed limit of oil and gas vehicles to 24 km/h (15 mph) and private vehicles to 40 km/h (25 mph) throughout the national seashore.

- Limiting the maximum number of trucks that can be in the national seashore each day.

- Prohibiting operation of oil and gas equipment along the beach at night.

- Requiring all oil and gas equipment to convoy as a group escorted by an NPS-trained observer of the endangered Kemp's ridley turtle (*Lepidochelys kempii*).

- Establishing a 152-m (500-ft) buffer around permanent freshwater ponds.

Shoreline Debris

Without modern lumberyards in Corpus Christi to frequent, Padre Ballí, Patrick Dunn, and others who built structures on Padre Island in historical times turned to the island itself for building materials. According to Sheire (1971), the Gulf of Mexico currents delivered a constant supply of hard and softwood boards of all lengths and widths for huts, kitchens, fences, and corrals. Furthermore, the sea provided furniture:

> Barrels with the tops removed and filled with sand became small stoves. Stools and chairs came in and found their way to the camps. Indeed, it is said Dunn furnished his headquarters home with furniture from the *Nicaragua*, an unlucky Mexican ship that stranded on Padre in 1912 or 1913. Tar barrels floated in and were melted to close holes. Other barrels collected rain water. Ropes of all sizes were used for a variety of purposes (Sheire 1971, p. 47).

The seashore's 1973 master plan highlights "fascinating" and "unusual" debris that drifts onto the beaches, which

visitors delighted in finding. In the 1990s the tone towards the island's generosity of offering up useful and interesting objects changed when sofas, refrigerators, televisions, chairs, buoys, and all types of plastics began to appear (National Park Service 1994). Mixed with benign items are ones potentially dangerous to humans and wildlife: fishing line, six-pack holders, nets, plastic bags, and hard plastics have killed turtles, birds, and other marine life (National Park Service 1994). Also, washed up on the beach are drums of toxic waste, medical supplies, military ordnance, broken glass, and sharp metal objects (National Park Service 1994).

The primary reason for trash accumulation on Padre Island is the convergence of currents along the Gulf of Mexico shoreline; thereby, the driver is geologic. The Loop Current enters the Gulf of Mexico through the Yucatan Channel and exits through the Florida Straits, moving north-northeast. Gyre Currents begin moving southward in October. These currents trap and later deposit trash onto the South Texas coastline, primarily around latitude 27°N. Significant for barrier-island development, this segment of the barrier island is the recipient of a continuous supply of sand and shell eroded from adjacent coastal sectors and transported by waves and longshore currents (Morton 1994). However, these currents also carry trash. Where currents collide, prevailing southeasterly winds push the debris onto Padre Island beaches.

The amount of trash on the beach is directly related to the strength, direction, and duration of the wind and the height of incoming tides, and, of course, human factors, such as the amount of trash that has been dumped into the Gulf of Mexico. Winds and tides also affect the movement of trash across the beach, from the shoreline to the backbeach and dunes. Old trash accumulates and becomes buried in the sand of the backbeach zone, for example in coppice dunes. Subsequent storms and high tides, combined with offshore winds, uncover and transport trash from the backbeach into the forebeach zone. Depending on the wind speed, direction, and duration, trash can be blown back into the Gulf of Mexico and subsequently float with the currents until redeposited onto the shoreline with the incoming high tides (Miller and Jones 2003).

According to Miller and Jones (2003), the most cost-effective and long-term solution to the beach-trash problem is to identify the sources and eliminate illegal dumping. The amount of garbage washing onto beaches at Padre Island National Seashore will not be reduced, nor will the overall problem in the Gulf of Mexico be adequately addressed, unless point sources are identified, violators are educated, and regulations such as the Marine Plastic Pollution Research and Control Act of 1988 (MARPOL V) are enforced.

Another geologically related issue concerning shoreline trash is the public perception that the oil and gas industry, in particular offshore platforms and rigs, is the primary culprit in dumping trash into the Gulf of Mexico (Ditton and Gramann 1987). However, according to a 10-year (1989–1998) study of shoreline trash, this is actually not the case (Miller and Jones 2003). Investigators of this study concluded that 9.2% of Padre Island trash originates with offshore oil and gas operations. By contrast, the shrimping industry was the primary violator and source of 80.8% of the trash collected according to the study.

Although not the first of its kind, the 10-year study, funded by six government agencies and trade groups, is the most exhaustive (Hart 2003). From March 1994 to February 1996 and March 1997 to February 1998, park crews collected trash daily from a 26-km (16-mi) stretch of shoreline in Padre Island National Seashore. Crews collected 376,396 pieces of trash, not including fragments. Researchers focused their analysis on 43 categories of debris, which they established during earlier surveys as the most commonly found along the shore.

Improvements to future studies would include working with port authorities and the Coast Guard to identify as many point sources as possible, then gathering distinctive items for each source, as well as determining how to categorize items that are not exclusive to any one source (e.g., bleach bottles and aluminum cans). Sources may also be terrestrial, such as coastal campsites and upland urban debris transported via runoff and flooding.

Grazing
Padre Island's coastal prairies, absence of chaparral, and natural boundaries for containing cattle made it an ideal location for cattle operations (National Park Service 1973) (fig. 6). Hence, for 166 years (1805–1971), Padre Island was cattle range:

- 1805–1846: Padre Nicolas Ballí cattle operation.

- 1846–1876: Various Mexican and American cattle operations, which provided roasts and steaks as military "mess" during the United States–Mexican War and Civil War; Richard King and Mifflin Kenedy ran cattle operations on the island from 1870 to 1886 (Callaway 1972).

- 1879–1971: Dunn family cattle operation.

Prior to cattle ranching, Padre Island was "as green as a garden"—an observation made by entrepreneur and rancher Mifflin Kenedy when he first saw the island (Price and Gunter 1942). Padre Island typically had a 4.5- to 15-m- (15- to 50-ft-) high, densely vegetated, foredune ridge behind the beach complex. In addition to grasses, vegetation included live oak (*Quercus fusiformis*) and brush (Price 1987). With vegetative cover depleted as a result of overgrazing, once-stabilized dunes moved across the landscape. Severe droughts also contributed to increased eolian material and transport across the wind-tidal flats and sedimentation into Laguna Madre (Price and Gunter 1942), but overgrazing was the main factor that resulted in prevailing winds blowing sand westward into the estuary (Prouty 1989).

The primary disturbances resulting from cattle grazing are changes in vegetation (species composition and percentage cover), destabilization of eolian features, and increased sedimentation onto the wind-tidal flats and

into Laguna Madre. Changes in vegetation led to changes in fauna (Rabalais 1977).

Although Prouty (1989) noted that the island was significantly revegetated during the 1970s and 1980s with higher rainfall and the elimination of grazing, various investigators have found that even after cattle were removed from the island, vegetation has failed to advance to its expected climactic stage (Kattner 1973; Drawe 1990), that is, mid- or even tall-grass climax vegetation dominated by seacoast bluestem (*Andropogon* spp. and *Schizachyrium* spp.), bushy bluestem (*Andropogon glomeratus*), and gulf beach panicum (*Panicum amarum*) (Drawe and Ortega 1996).

Wind Energy
Kenedy Ranch, on the mainland across from Padre Island National Seashore, clocks some of the highest wind speeds along the entire Gulf of Mexico. Average wind speeds are 28.4 km/h (17.7 mph) at the site (Babcock & Brown 2008). Kenedy Ranch now hosts a wind power facility with 118 wind turbines that each generates 2.4 megawatts of electricity. The turbines are 13 km (8 mi) inland from the Gulf of Mexico and 8 km (5 mi) west of Laguna Madre (The John G & Marie Stella Kenedy Memorial Foundation 2008).

Wind energy development is addressed in a geologic resources inventory for two reasons: (1) eolian features and processes are a geologic resource to be protected throughout the National Park System, and (2) the NPS Geologic Resources Division provides policy and technical support to parks contending with energy development (both renewable and nonrenewable) within and adjacent to their boundaries. While the National Park Service supports the use of renewable energy, it wants to ensure that the appropriate technologies are used in the appropriate locations (McCoy 2009). At Padre Island National Seashore, the National Park Service has concerns about the impacts of wind power facilities on migrating bird and marine species, as well as changes in fishing pressure (i.e., bait fish congregate near structures for food and shelter, thereby attracting predator species), changes in habitat as a result of transmission lines (i.e., alterations in magnetic field may affect sea turtle migration), and terrestrial impacts of routing a right-of-way across the park to access the power grid (Darrell Echols, National Park Service, written communication, July 6, 2009).

In 2009, the Natural Resource Science and Stewardship Directorate (NRSS) and the Natural Resources Advisory Group, consisting of park and regional representatives, drafted an action plan for energy development. The plan is an initial step to increase the National Park Service's capacity to respond more effectively and influence outcomes to protect parks.

Monitoring at the Kenedy Ranch facility could test the effectiveness of implemented mitigation measures; increase understanding of impacts on avian, terrestrial, and marine species; and help determine whether particular technologies are preventing avian mortality.

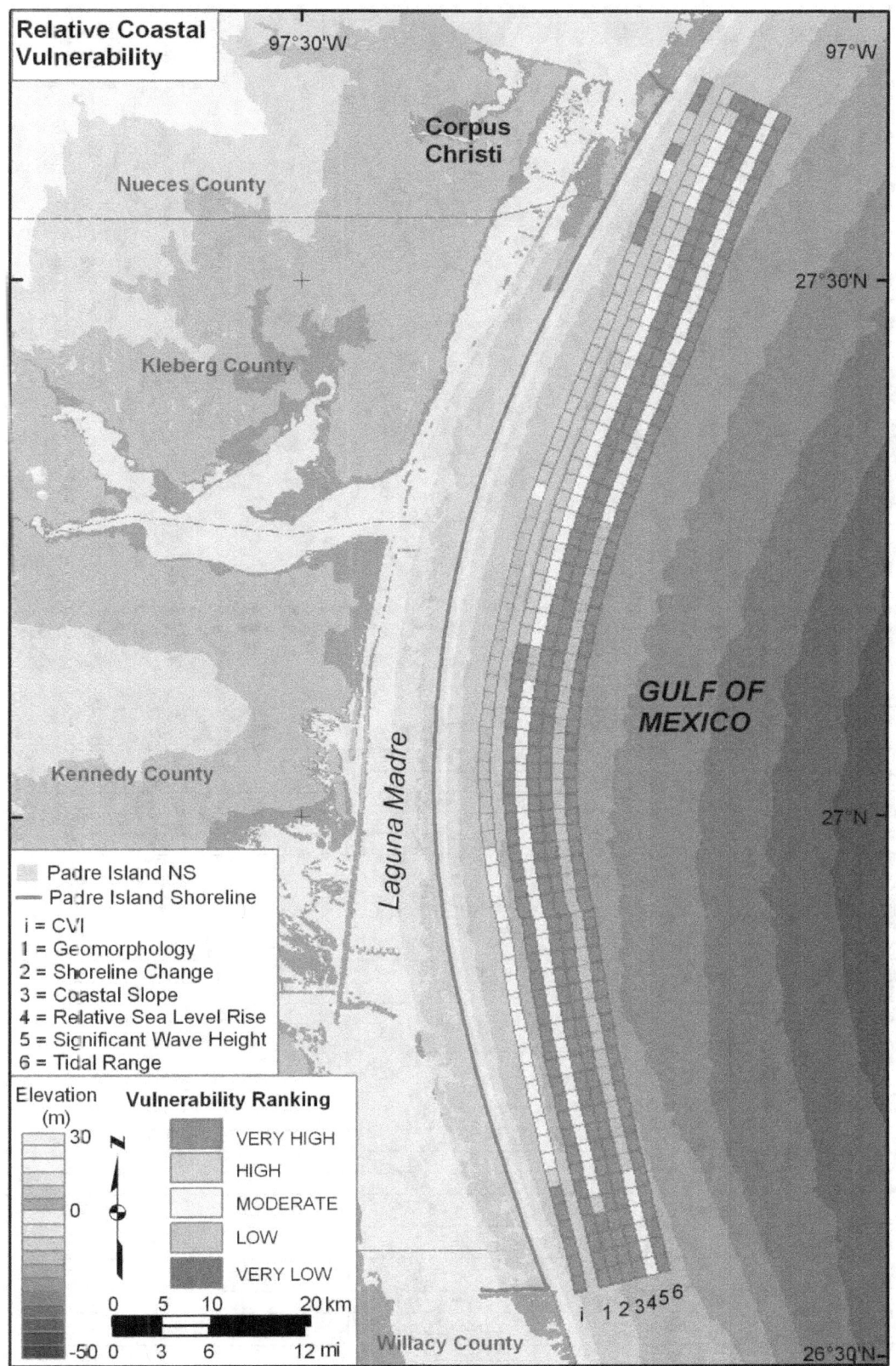

Relative Coastal Vulnerability

Corpus Christi

Nueces County

Kleberg County

Kennedy County

Laguna Madre

GULF OF MEXICO

97°30'W

97°W

27°30'N

27°N

26°30'N

Padre Island NS
Padre Island Shoreline
i = CVI
1 = Geomorphology
2 = Shoreline Change
3 = Coastal Slope
4 = Relative Sea Level Rise
5 = Significant Wave Height
6 = Tidal Range

Elevation (m)

Vulnerability Ranking

VERY HIGH
HIGH
MODERATE
LOW
VERY LOW

30

0

-50

0   5   10   20 km

0   3   6   12 mi

i 1 2 3 4 5 6

Willacy County

Figure 2. Coastal vulnerability index. Investigators classified 17% of the Gulf of Mexico shoreline at Padre Island National Seashore as having very high vulnerability to future sea-level rise, 28% as having high vulnerability, 29% as having moderate vulnerability, and 26% as having low vulnerability. Image from Pendelton et al. (2004). Used by permission of the author, R. L. Beavers.

Figure 3. Blowing sand. Although a natural process and necessary for dune formation, mitigation of blowing sand requires many hours of maintenance at Padre Island National Seashore, for example along the road to Malaquite Beach shown in the photograph. National Park Service photograph.

Table 2. Hurricanes making landfall near Padre Island (1900–2010)

Name	Date	Landfall	Category	Wind speed km/h	Wind speed mph
Dolly	July 23, 2008	South Padre Island	1	138	86
Bret	August 22, 1999	Padre Island	3	185	115
Gilbert	September 17, 1988	South of Brownsville	4	217	135
Allen	August 10, 1980	Port Mansfield	3	185	115
Celia	August 3, 1970	Corpus Christi	3	201	125
Beulah	September 20, 1967	Brownsville	3	217	135
Carla	September 11, 1961	Port Lavaca	4	233	145
Number 3	July 25, 1934	Rockport	2	161	100
Number 11	September 4, 1933	Brownsville	3	201	125
Number 2	September 14, 1919	Corpus Christi	4	230	143
Number 6	August 18, 1916	Corpus Christi	4	217	135
Number 2	June 26, 1902	Port Lavaca	1	129	80

Source: Roth (2009).

Note: Roth (2009) gave unnamed storms a name (e.g., "number 3") based on its occurrence in a particular year. Category is 1 to 5 on the Saffir-Simpson hurricane intensity scale.

Table 3. Requirements for renourishment at Bird Island Basin

Estimated project lifespan, in years	Distance offshore Meters	Distance offshore Feet	Volume Cubic meters	Volume Cubic yards
\multicolumn{5}{c}{*Fine sand, 2.75φ (locally derived)*}				
5	5.0	16.4	1,802	2,357
10	10.0	32.8	2,827	3,698
20	19.9	65.6	5,483	7,172
\multicolumn{5}{c}{*Medium sand, 2.0–1.5 φ (quarry derived)*}				
5	5.0	16.4	1,391–1,213	1,820–1,587
10	10.0	32.8	2,440–2,255	3,192–2,949
20	19.9	65.6	4,751–4,636	6,214–6,063

Data from Smith-Engle et al. (2006, 2007).

Figure 4. Vehicle impacts. Beach driving is a popular activity at Padre Island National Seashore. Regulations serve to minimize potential impacts and disturbance to resources. Note speed limit sign. National Park Service photograph by Rebecca Beavers (NPS Geologic Resources Division).

Figure 5. Oil and gas operations. The National Park Service evaluates operations plans from authorized operators and has developed regulations and mitigation measures to allow access to nonfederal oil and gas resources beneath the park while minimizing impacts to visitors and resources. This well, drilled in 2007, was a short-lived producer and is now plugged. Reclamation is ongoing (Pat O'Dell, NPS Geologic Resources Division, personal communication. September 20, 2010). National Park Service photograph courtesy Pat O'Dell.

Figure 6. Grasslands of Padre Island National Seashore. Padre Island's coastal prairies are dominated by bluestems (*Andropogon* spp. and *Schizachyrium* sp.), sea oats (*Uniola paniculata*), and *Paspalum* spp. National Park Service photograph.

Geologic Features and Processes

This section describes the most prominent and distinctive geologic features and processes in Padre Island National Seashore.

Wind Activity

Wind is perhaps the most important geologic agent at Padre Island National Seashore because its effects are both direct and indirect (Morton and McGowen 1980). Directly, winds move sand through eolian processes. Depending on whether overall conditions are wet or dry, winds build or move dunes, accrete or erode wind-tidal flats, and inflate or deflate swales and depressions (Withers et al. 2004). Indirectly, wind stresses generate waves, currents, and tides that circulate water in Laguna Madre, flood the wind-tidal flats, and control sediment transport onto and off of beaches and wind-tidal flats.

In many areas of Padre Island National Seashore, overwash does not reach the lagoon side of the island; deposition stops on the beach or interdunal areas. Hence, eolian transport and deposition are important for building the wind-tidal flats and helping the island keep pace with rising sea level (see "Coastal Vulnerability") (Courtney Schupp, National Park Service, written communication, September 29, 2009).

Wave and Current Activity

More than 12,000 waves break on the shore daily at Padre Island National Seashore (Weise and White 1980). Gulf waves breaking along the shoreline are usually less than 1 m (3.3 ft) high, but some reach heights of 2 m (6.6 ft) during fall, winter, and spring storms (Hill and Hunter 1976). Waves, large and small, build the island lagoonward in both subtle and dramatic ways. Each wave lifts sediment, shifting and sorting every grain. Little by little, daily wave swash transports sediment to and from the shore. More dramatically, storm-surge waves transport sediment across the island in washover channels and fans.

The lifting action of waves makes sand available for currents to transport sediment parallel to the shoreline, a process called longshore drift. Winds blowing into a concave shoreline, such as the South Texas coast, produce waves that approach a beach at an angle. These waves generate currents along the shore, which in turn generate longshore drift. The longshore currents of the Texas coast include those along the North Texas coastline, which move southward, and those along the South Texas coastline, which move northward. In the vicinity of Padre Island National Seashore, these currents transport sediment from two source areas—the Rio Grande to the south and the Brazos–Colorado River system to the north.

Quartz is the primary constituent of Padre Island sediment, but particular minerals can be diagnostic of source areas: Rio Grande sediments (to the south) are derived from a variety of rocks characterized by the accessory minerals hornblende and pyroxene. To the north, sedimentary rocks dominate river basins, and garnet, tourmaline, rutile, staurolite, and zircon characterize heavy minerals in these sediments. In addition, sediments supplied in the Brazos–Colorado River drainage system have a considerable amount of green hornblende derived from igneous and metamorphic rocks in the Central Basin (Llano Uplift) of Texas (Bullard 1942; van Andel 1960).

Rio Grande sediments are carried northward along Padre Island by longshore drift and converge in a transition zone with Brazos–Colorado River sediments carried southward in the same manner. In addition to lithologic differences, grain-size distribution on Padre Island shows that fine-grained sediment comes from the northern source, coarse-grained sediment from the southern source, and both fine- and coarse-grained sediment from the transition zone (Brezina 2004). This zone of transition and convergence is the site of the largest accumulations of heavy minerals, shells, and sand (see "Shells").

Tidal Activity

At Padre Island, meteorological tides (i.e., wind-driven tides) are much more important than astronomical tides (i.e., those produced by the gravitational pull of the moon and the sun) (Tunnell 2002a). Commonly, wind-induced changes in water level are larger than those caused by astronomical tides. For example, an 80-km/h (50-mph) wind produced a 46-cm (18-in) drop in lagoon water level in an hour (National Park Service 2007). Such dramatic wind-induced drops in water level can leave boats stranded in Laguna Madre.

Wind stress coupled with changes in barometric pressure often raises or lowers water levels on Gulf of Mexico beaches as much as 1 m (3.3 ft) compared to the predicted astronomical tides (Morton and Speed 1998), which average about 40 cm (16 in) (Weise and White 1980) and range from 45 cm to 60 cm (18 in to 24 in) (Morton and McGowen 1980). Depending on the time of the month, astronomical tides in the Gulf of Mexico are diurnal (vary systematically and repeat themselves once daily) or mixed (vary irregularly twice daily). Variations in astronomical tides are considerably lower in bays and lagoons (Morton and McGowen 1980). Wind tides on Laguna Madre are in the range of 0.3 m to 1.2 m (1 ft to 4 ft) (Rusnak 1960).

These parameters classify the Gulf of Mexico as a "microtidal," low-energy coastline. Such coastlines are essentially synonymous with storm-dominated coasts because the expended energy and geologic shaping of the land accomplished during storms overwhelm daily processes (Morton and McGowen 1980).

Barrier Island System

A series of distinct geomorphic provinces comprises Padre Island (fig. 7). These provinces are the physical outcome of wind, wave, and tidal activity; vegetation also plays a significant role. The map units presented on the digital geologic map for Padre Island National Seashore (i.e., Gibeaut and Tremblay 2005) can be grouped into these provinces. Although some map units are part of more than one geomorphic province (e.g., active dunes), generally speaking, starting from the Gulf of Mexico and working towards Laguna Madre, the provinces are as follows: beach (see "Map Unit Properties Table," unit B1), coppice dunes (unit B2), fore-island dune ridge (unit B3), active dunes (unit B10), stabilized dunes (unit B5a), vegetated and sparsely vegetated barrier flats (units B4 and B5), and back-island sand flats (B11). Other sand flats (unit B8a) fringe vegetated barrier flats and coppice-dune fields in the back-island area. Brackish and fresh marshes and ponds (units B4a–d and B9) form in barrier flats and storm washover channels (unit B7). In the southern part of the national seashore, washover channels slice across the island and associated fans (unit B7a) are deposited on wind-tidal flats. Transitional between the barrier island and lagoon systems are wind-deflation flats (unit B8) or troughs.

Nearshore Zone

Often included in classification systems of barrier-island morphology is the nearshore zone (Rebecca Beavers, Geologic Resources Division, e-mail message, September 1, 2010). The nearshore zone is represented by the "upper shoreface" and "forebeach" of Weise and White (1980) (see fig. 6), and as part of the beach (unit B1) on the digital geologic map for Padre Island National Seashore. According to Gibeaut and Tremblay (2005), the beach (B1) unit is bounded to the east by marine open waters of the Gulf of Mexico and landward by a prominent fore-island dune ridge. The gulfward shoreline was mapped using 2000 LIDAR (light detection and ranging) data. To complete this classification scheme, the "offshore zone" is the open water that lies seaward of the nearshore zone.

The nearshore zone is a significant part of the barrier-island environment because it is the site of sediment transport, both longshore (parallel to the shoreline) and cross shore (perpendicular, onto and off of the shoreline). Subjected to the unending onslaught of waves, the nearshore zone is divided into "subzones" based on wave behavior. The nearshore zone extends from where waves begin to break (breaker zone) across where most of the wave energy is dissipated (surf zone) to where the beach is covered and uncovered repeatedly by each surging wave (swash zone) (Pinet 1992).

Beach

Padre Island National Seashore is traditionally subdivided into five named beaches (fig. 1). North Beach extends for 1.8 km (1.1 mi) from the national seashore's northern boundary to a row of posts that crosses the beach and marks the boundary with Closed (Malaquite) Beach. Closed Beach extends for 7.2 km (4.5 mi) to a row of pylons that marks its southern boundary. Closed

Beach incorporates the Malaquite Beach facilities, including the visitor center and campground. Closed Beach's southern boundary is the zero point for measuring distances on the remaining 96 km (60 mi) of beach within Padre Island National Seashore (see fig. 1). South Beach extends from Closed Beach's southern boundary approximately 11 km (7 mi) to the beginning of Little Shell Beach, which is not marked by any posts or pylons. Little Shell Beach extends from the southern boundary of Closed Beach approximately 11 km (7 mi) to milepost 12. Big Shell Beach extends from approximately 27 km (17 mi) to 45 km (28 mi) south of Closed Beach. As the names imply, the seashells making up Little Shell Beach are smaller than the shells found at Big Shell Beach (see "Shells"). The beaches south of Big Shell Beach are not named and are usually designated only by their distances from Closed Beach's southern boundary.

Padre Island beaches are composed of fine sand, which coarsens slightly from north to south (Hayes 1965). The primary constituent is the mineral quartz, but the sand also contains rock fragments, the mineral feldspar, and heavy minerals, such as hornblende, pyroxene, garnet, staurolite, rutile, zircon, and tourmaline (Bullard 1942). In addition to these terrestrial components, shell and shell fragments make up varying percentages of the total beach sediment. The highest concentrations of shell (as much as 80%) occur where longshore currents converge between Big Shell and Little Shell beaches (Weise and White 1980).

Geomorphologists often divide the beach province into two zones: forebeach (or "foreshore beach") and backbeach (or "backshore beach") (Weise and White 1980; see fig. 7). The forebeach slopes gently towards the Gulf of Mexico and is subject to the daily swash of waves (fig. 8). As a result, sedimentary structures in the beach environment are primarily seaward-dipping laminations produced by wave swash. Commonly, concentrations of heavy minerals and shell fragments accentuate the laminations (Morton and McGowen 1980). Burrowing organisms on the beach tend to destroy primary stratigraphic forms, however. The backbeach and upper forebeach are dominated by the burrowing ghost crab (*Ocypode quadrata*), while ghost shrimp (*Callianassa islagrande*) characterize the lower forebeach (Hunter et al. 1972). Scientists use variations in burrow morphology, including spatial density, size, and shape, to designate subenvironments of the beach (Brezina 2004).

The apex of the forebeach—the berm crest—divides the forebeach from the backbeach. Generally, the backbeach is either horizontal or slopes gently landward, creating a shallow trough between the berm crest and fore-island dune ridge. Rills formed by flood runoff may produce scour and fill (sedimentary structures) in the backbeach zone, but generally surfaces are smooth and internal stratification is faint (Morton and McGowen 1980).

During fair weather, the backshore is inactive with respect to wave swash, although the wind continually moves sand landward in this zone (Hill and Hunter 1987). However, because of the dampness of the sand due to its low elevation, wind erosion seldom lowers the level of the backshore by more than a few centimeters. Wave swash does reach the backshore several times a year, mostly during winter storms, but only hurricanes cause severe damage in this zone (Hill and Hunter 1987).

The sand eroded from the beach during storms is deposited in nearshore areas and is gradually carried back to the beach by normal wave activity (Hunter et al. 1972). Higher than normal waves and tides move coarser sediments and shell fragments onto the backbeach. Storm surge transports coarser material farther landward through storm washover channels (i.e., breaches in the fore-island dune ridge). After initial storm deposition, a lag deposit of coarse shell fragments may form on the backbeach in response to eolian removal ("winnowing") of finer sediments.

Coppice Dunes

As a result of prevailing southeasterly winds, coppice dunes form in the backbeach zone and fringe the edges of active back-island dune fields. Sediment composing coppice dunes is fine beach sand that has blown landward and collected around clumps of vegetation and the wind shadows behind them (Weise and White 1980). Coppice dunes in the backbeach form a narrow band of sandy mounds that parallel the beach for miles. In the southern part of the national seashore, where the foredune ridge is absent or segmented, broader coppice dune fields extend landward from the beach (Weise and White 1980). Normally, coppice dunes remain small, less than 0.9 m (3 ft) high, but they may grow to 1.8 m (6 ft) or more if the vegetation that helps to build them remains healthy and is not destroyed by storms or human activities. Larger coppice dunes may merge and become part of the fore-island dune ridge (Weise and White 1980).

Fore-Island Dune Ridge

The fore-island dune ridge—also referred to as the "foredune ridge" or simply "foredunes"—is immediately landward of the backbeach and aligned parallel to the shoreline (figs. 8 and 9). These dunes protect the barrier flats from the full onslaught of tropical storms.

Foredune sediments on Padre Island consist of very well sorted, fine and very fine sands, which are blown from the backbeach and stabilized by vegetation. Climate, soil moisture, and soil temperature affect the growth of vegetation and, therefore, the stability of foredunes. The drier, southern parts of Padre Island have low foredunes. By contrast, elevations of large foredunes on Big Shell Beach reach 15 m (50 ft) where denser vegetation traps sand. Interestingly, foredunes in the area of longshore drift convergence (i.e., around latitude 27°N or mile marker 30) show a distinct correlation between increased or maximum amount of shell fragments on the beach and the location of high, continuous foredunes (Watson 1968). Low dunes or storm washover channels correspond to local minima in shell fragment percentages. This positive correlation does not occur elsewhere on Padre Island, however (Brezina 2004).

In addition to vegetation, foredune development and foredune height are directly related to sediment supply (Brezina 2004). Rivers are the primary source of sand for building barriers and beaches in the western Gulf of Mexico (Morton 1994). According to Hayes (1963), the source of sand in beaches and dunes along the southern end of Padre Island is the Rio Grande. The Nueces, Colorado, and several other rivers are the sources of sand to the north. When rainfall and associated fluvial activity decreased in the early Holocene, sand supplied to the beaches also decreased (see "Geologic History"). More recently, watershed development, such as construction of surface-water reservoirs, flood-control structures, and freshwater diversions, have resulted in additional reductions in sand supply (Morton 1994).

Like height, width of the fore-island dune ridge varies along the island. Generally, the ridge is about 60 m to 90 m (200 ft to 300 ft) wide; however, in areas where the foredunes became blowouts and later stabilized landward, the dune ridge is wider, as much as 370 m (1,200 ft) across (Weise and White 1980).

Active Dunes

Active dunes exemplify barrier-island migration. Active dunes occur as fore-island blowout dunes or in back-island dune fields. Where vegetation is destroyed, the fore-island dune ridge is vulnerable to erosion by the strong southeasterly winds (fig. 10). Sand is blown from the dune ridge across the barrier flat in a northwesterly direction. The result is a blowout dune complex, composed of rapidly changing dune forms. The sediment in these blowout dunes is mostly fine, well-sorted sand derived from fore-island dunes. Stratification resulting from dune migration consists principally of horizontal-to-inclined plane-parallel laminae, climbing-ripple laminae, and ripple laminae (Hunter 1977). Predominant wind directions cause cross-strata to dip northwest (Morton and McGowen 1980). As blowout dunes migrate, they may either become stabilized by grasses or merge with a back-island dune field (Weise and White 1980).

In the northern part of the national seashore, fine sand is supplied to the back-island dune fields by the migrating blowout dunes. In the southern part, sand reworked from sediments that washed into the back-island area during storms largely supplies the back-island dunes. Presently, neither washover deposits nor large blowout dunes occur in the central part of the national seashore; as a result, the back-island area is starved of the sand necessary to build large dune fields there. In this part of the national seashore, vegetated barrier flats have replaced what were once dune fields (Weise and White 1980).

Stabilized Dunes

In many parts of Padre Island National Seashore, elongated and parabolic-shaped dunes covered in vegetation extend lagoonward from the foredune ridge. These dunes, as much as 6 m (20 ft) high, were once active blowout dunes that originated at the dune ridge. After migrating some distance towards Laguna Madre, they became stabilized by vegetation (fig. 11) (Weise and White 1980). If the grass cover is destroyed, the dunes may be reactivated and begin migrating again.

Because the sediments of the stabilized blowout dunes were derived from the fore-island dune ridge, they resemble foredune sediments. The stabilized deposits include fine, well-sorted sand. Nearest the fore-island area, they contain small shells and shell fragments that were blown or washed from the beach (Weise and White 1980).

Barrier Flats

Vegetated (and sparsely vegetated) barrier flats are the most common terrestrial environment at Padre Island National Seashore (Gibeaut and Tremblay 2005). They spread behind the fore-island dune ridge, gently sloping towards Laguna Madre. They have little topographic relief and commonly lie less than 1.5 m (5 ft) above mean water level (Leatherman 1988). According to Weise and White (1980), the more sparsely vegetated barrier flats are areas where grasses have been established recently and have not had enough time or moisture to develop a dense cover. These areas were recently eroded by wind and have supplied sand to the active dunes. If rainfall is sufficient, most of the sparsely vegetated flats will evolve into more heavily vegetated flats (Weise and White 1980). The majority of sparsely vegetated barrier flats occur on the windward (southeast) edge of migrating dune fields.

Most barrier flats on the Gulf of Mexico coast of South Texas have some percentage of barren or minimally vegetated deflation flats. Wind-deflation flats are the low areas left behind migrating dune fields. Eolian removal of sand and finer sediments deflates these surfaces, often down to the water table.

Barrier flats can host ponds and marshes, which occur in troughs associated with deflation flats. Troughs are generally linear and are located in areas through which dunes have migrated. Although these troughs were originally floored in sandy sediments, ponding and associated growth of marsh vegetation promoted deposition of mud and plant debris. Organic debris is mixed or interlayered with episodic additions of eolian sands (Brezina 2004). On Padre Island, accumulations of organic matter and fine sediments are limited to ponds and marshes (Weise and White 1980), and pond deposits are the only barrier-island sediments that have low permeability and high water-holding capacity (McGowen et al. 1976).

Back-Island Sand Flats

A sand flat is one possible last stage in the life of a dune field (Weise and White 1980). Non-vegetated sand flats fringe barrier flats and coppice-dune fields in the back-island area. Sand within the flats commonly forms small, rapidly migrating dunes. As the sand continues to spread and dunes become smaller, the elevation of the sand flat is reduced sufficiently so that the area is flooded by normal wind tides, and the environment evolves into a wind-tidal flat (Weise and White 1980).

Storm Washover Channels and Fans

Created and reopened during hurricanes, washover channels provide a conduit for Gulf of Mexico waters to freshen the hypersaline waters of Laguna Madre (National Park Service 2000). Natural, storm washover channels as much as 213 m (700 ft) wide cut through the dune ridge (Weise and White 1980). Sediments eroded from the beach and adjacent dunes are spread lagoonward over the wind-tidal flats, forming fan-shaped deposits called washover fans. The fans are lobes of sand and shell having very low relief that are deposited where the washover channels widen and the storm waters lose velocity. Storm waters also carry some sediment parallel to the shoreline along the wind-deflation flats (Hayes 1965). Where artificial channels, such as Mansfield Channel, connect the Gulf of Mexico and Laguna Madre (and in other locations with natural inlets), hurricane surge may produce strong currents that dramatically raise lagoon water levels. As the hurricane passes, elevated lagoon waters, which are produced by surge and winds, create currents that flow toward the Gulf of Mexico and transport sediments back through washover channels, artificial passes, and natural inlets (Weise and White 1980).

All washover channels eroded during recent hurricanes occur in the southern part of the national seashore. These are likely to be reactivated during the next large storm. Washover channels are much more prominent in the southern part of the national seashore because the dune ridge is low and segmented as a result of (1) higher shoreline erosion rates, which reduce the amount of sediment available for dune construction, and (2) a drier climate and consequently much less vegetation to bind the sand (Weise and White 1980).

The first washover channel is about 27 km (17 mi) south of Yarborough Pass (see fig. 1). Older, healed washovers are located approximately 6.4 km (4 mi) south of Yarborough Pass and 14 km (9 mi) south of Malaquite Beach. These relict channels are not mapped as hurricane washovers on the digital geologic map of Padre Island National Seashore, but rather as the various environments that have developed in them. Nevertheless, the stratigraphy of Padre Island National Seashore, in this case relict washover channels and fans, documents past hurricanes as part of the geologic record. According to Suter and Maynard (1983), relatively thin deposits consisting of numerous coalescing washovers represent low-profile barriers in the stratigraphic record. Thicker sand bodies corresponding to high-profile barriers occur along strike.

Major washover channels eroded below mean sea level may continue to pond water after normal nearshore processes have reconstructed the beach across the channel mouths, severing their connection with Gulf of Mexico waters. Most ponds that form in the deepest parts of the washover channels exist only briefly. Where channels are scoured below the water table, however, the ponds retain brackish water. Thin algal mats develop around the edges of the ponds and in other moist parts of the channels between storms (Weise and White 1980).

Washover fans that are deposited over the wind-tidal flats provide a source of sand for the formation of back-island dune fields (Boker 1953). In some areas, for example along the southern end of the national seashore, "pavements" composed of large shells and shell fragments form lagoonward of the backbeach and fore-island dunes. These deposits are evidence of storm surge and the effect of subsequent eolian processes, which deflate the surface and leave the shell concentrated there (Weise and White 1980). Hayes (1967) discovered shells 4.0 km (2.5 mi) landward of the beach as a result of Hurricane Carla's surge.

Lagoon System

The lagoon system includes wind-tidal flats (units L1, L2, and L3), lagoon-margin sand (unit L5), and grassflats (unit L6). Sand and shell berms (natural islands; unit L4) and spoil mounds (unit M1, M2, and M3) occur in Laguna Madre itself.

Laguna Madre is the largest hypersaline estuary in the world, extending 445 km (277 mi) from the mouth of Corpus Christi Bay, Texas, to the Rio Soto La Marina, Tamaulipas, Mexico. The maximum width of the lagoon is approximately 16 km (10 mi); however, its width in many places fluctuates considerably with the height of wind-generated tides. The lagoon is widest during highest wind tides, which produce maximum flooding of the vast adjacent tidal flats (Weise and White 1980).

The depth of Laguna Madre ranges from a subaerial land bridge to a submerged bottom, where the muddy sand lies at depths of 2.4 m (8 ft) (Weise and White 1980). According to Morton (1994), lagoon sediments are less than 3 m (10 ft) thick and overlie relatively stiff mud of the Rio Grande delta (see "Geologic History"). The shallowest parts of the lagoon are in the central part of the national seashore, in the Land Cut, which forms a land bridge between Padre Island and mainland Texas. Also known as the "Salt Flats," "Saltillo Flats," "Kenedy Flats," and "Laguna Madre Flats," "Land Cut" was probably coined when the Gulf Intracoastal Waterway was excavated through this area (Withers et al. 2004).

The Land Cut was formed over several thousand years as a result of sediment transport from Padre Island to the mainland (Morton and McGowen 1980). Hurricanes and tropical storms, in conjunction with eolian processes, moved sediment from Padre Island landward into Laguna Madre (Morton and McGowen 1980).

Padre Island all but isolates Laguna Madre, separating it from the Gulf of Mexico and restricting seawater flow into and out of the lagoon. In addition, no rivers flow into the lagoon. Most fresh water enters the system during infrequent, but often massive, storms, when several inches to several feet of rain can fall within a few days. Although these storms are often associated with summer tropical weather systems, they can occur at any time of the year (Withers et al. 2004). During such events, sheet flow in the area of the Land Cut also provides a source of freshwater (Brown et al. 1977).

Storm surge and eolian processes contribute sand and shell fragments to wind-tidal flats; mud is derived from adjacent lagoons. Sediment transport created extensive wind-tidal flats on the periphery of Laguna Madre, and the flats are subject to flooding by wind tides (see "Wind Activity" and "Tidal Activity"). Wind-tidal flats occupy the entire lagoon in the vicinity of Land Cut (Weise and White 1980).

Frequently inundated by Laguna-Madre waters driven by the wind, some parts of the flats support extensive mats of blue-green algae; the algae thrive when wet but die, crack, and peel when dry. Desiccation coupled with heaving from biogenic gases and air trapped beneath the algal mats produces chaotic and contorted bedding. In addition, biochemical precipitates of calcium carbonate are interlaminated with algal mats near the surface (Morton and McGowen 1980).

Evaporite, Fulgurite, and Oolite

Amidst so much sand, seeing a rock at Padre Island National Seashore is a memorable experience. The national seashore hosts three distinctive types of rocks: evaporite, fulgurite, and oolite. Rock specimens, especially those as unique as the following, might be targets for unauthorized collecting. However, no studies of human behavior regarding collection of rocks and minerals have been conducted at Padre Island National Seashore, and it is not known whether theft of these limited resources is a problem at the national seashore.

Evaporite

Bladelike crystals of gypsum (calcium sulfate) form in the wind-tidal flats of Laguna Madre. Gypsum is an evaporite rock, which forms as a result of extensive or total evaporation of a saline solution. At Padre Island National Seashore, gypsum crystals form when high-salinity waters periodically flood the wind-tidal flats and seep into the underlying sediments. Gypsum is precipitated in the pore spaces of the sandy substrate, cementing the sand grains and forming gypsum-sand crystals (Fisk 1959). These crystals grow larger with each successive flooding, infiltration, and precipitation (Masson 1955). Crystals increase in size with depth; they are less than 2.5 cm (1 in) in length near the top of the water table and more than 0.3 m (1 ft) at a depth of 3.7 m (12 ft) below sea level (Fisk 1959).

Gypsum occurs in three forms at Padre Island: (1) clear, amber-colored blades or crystals (selenite); (2) gray, sand-textured blades or crystals; and (3) small, light-colored, sand-textured rosettes (fig. 12) (Tunnell 2002b). Clusters of rosettes—also called "sand roses" or "gypsum roses"—can reach 50 cm (20 in) in length and weigh as much as 11 kg (24 lb) (McBride et al. 1991).

The Laguna Madre area is the only place in Texas where gypsum rosettes occur (fig. 7), namely on both sides of the Gulf Intracoastal Waterway in the vicinity of the Land Cut, and along Mansfield Channel (Tunnell 2002b). When channels were dredged across the flats, the crystals were deposited along with other dredge material in piles. Over time, wind and rain erode the sandy sediment, leaving the crystals and rosettes exposed on the surface (Tunnell 2002b).

Fulgurite

When lightning hits sand, it can fuse the particles together, forming fulgurite (fig. 12). Likely places for lightning strike are points of highest elevation, which in the case of Padre Island National Seashore are dune ridges. Lightning penetrates the ground and turns the sand into glass, which forms in the path of the strike, creating branches or rods below ground and crusts on the surface. Fusion also may vaporize the center of fulgurite, resulting in a tube.

Usually fulgurite is between 2 cm (1 in) and 5 cm (2 in) in diameter, but the national seashore's museum collection contains a few exceptionally rare specimens that are 10 cm (4 in) across. Workers discovered these pieces during the construction of the Malaquite Visitor Center. Specimens are now displayed at the visitor center, where they can serve as a reminder to visitors about the importance of staying off the dunes, particularly as storms approach.

Oolite

Resembling fish roe, oolite is a sedimentary rock, usually limestone, made of ooliths—round or oval grains formed by accretion around a nucleus of shell fragment, algal pellet, or sand grain. These laminated grains may reach diameters of 2 mm (0.08 in.), but 0.5 mm to 1 mm (0.02 in to 0.04 in) is common. Oolite is usually formed of calcium carbonate but may consist of dolomite, silica, or other minerals.

The classic interpretation of oolite formation suggests that wave-agitated water is necessary for layers to accrete. However, the oolites in Laguna Madre defy this interpretation. Formation in the quiet waters of Laguna Madre proves that high energy is not essential, at least for irregular forms (Tunnell 2002b).

Like gypsum crystals, Laguna Madre is the only place where oolite is found in Texas. It is forming on the Laguna Madre shoreline just north of the Point of Rocks at the mouth of Baffin Bay and near two submerged sand bars between Baffin Bay and Padre Island (Tunnell 2002b).

Shells

Approximately 350 species of shell-bearing organisms occur along the Texas coast (Andrews 1972). About half of these are very minute and easily overlooked by the casual beachcomber, but collectors have found 37 species of bivalves (e.g., clams, oysters, scallops, and mussels) and gastropods (e.g., snails or limpets) at Padre Island National Seashore (National Park Service 2006c). Specimens include bivalves such as spiny jewel box

(*Arcinella arcinella*), bay scallop (*Argopecten irradians*), and incongruous ark (*Anadara brasiliana* Lamarck) (fig. 8) and gastropods such as rock shell (*Thais haemastoma floridana* Conrad), sundial (*Architectonica noblis* Roding), and lightning whelk (*Busycon contrarium* Conrad) (fig. 13). The most sought after shell on the Texas coast is the beautifully spiraled Mitchell's wentletrap (*Amaea mitchelli* Dall), which washes ashore only on the Texas and Mexico shorelines of the Gulf of Mexico (Andrews 1972).

Two distinct shell assemblages occur on Padre Island beaches. Northern beaches in the national seashore are almost entirely composed of small surf clams, primarily *Donax variabilis* Say but also *Donax tumida* Say. Southern beaches are characterized by the bivalve mollusks southern quahog (*Mercenaria campechiensis* Gmelin) and the large clams *Eontia ponderosa* Say and *Echinochama arcinella* Linne. Either dead or living small surf clams (*Donax* sp.) are generally absent except for a small colony about 32 km (20 mi) north of Mansfield Channel (Watson 1968). Ark shells (e.g., *Andara braziliana* Lamarck, *Andara ovalis* Bruguiere, and *Andara baughmani* Hertlein) are common throughout the extent of Padre Island and do not exhibit any particular pattern of distribution. The transition zone between north and south has a lower total percentage of shells than do flanking areas, which have slightly increased numbers of the ark (*Andara*) species. Percentage of shell species and degree of abrasion suggest that the large-clam (*Mercenaria-Eontia-Echinochama*) assemblage has a southern source and is transported to the north and that the small surf-clam (*Donax*) assemblage has a northern source and is transported to the south (Watson 1968).

Following a life span within the surf zone, *Donax* is transported southward by longshore drift to accumulate on Little Shell Beach. Large-clam (*Mercenaria-Eontia-Echinochama*) shells are abraded and not present as fresh specimens on Big Shell Beach (Watson 1968). The shells on Little Shell and Big Shell beaches are much abraded as a result of continuous reworking by wave action (Morton 1977). In addition, the large-clam (*Mercenaria*) shells are commonly highly discolored. These observations suggest accumulation of shell fragments due to differential sorting by wave energy and not a locally rich population. The discoloration might also suggest an older, reworked shell assemblage, possibly subject to burial prior to accumulation in a beach environment (Brezina 2004).

Unoccupied sea shells may be collected in limited quantities within the national seashore for noncommercial use. No other natural or cultural resources may be collected without a research permit.

West East

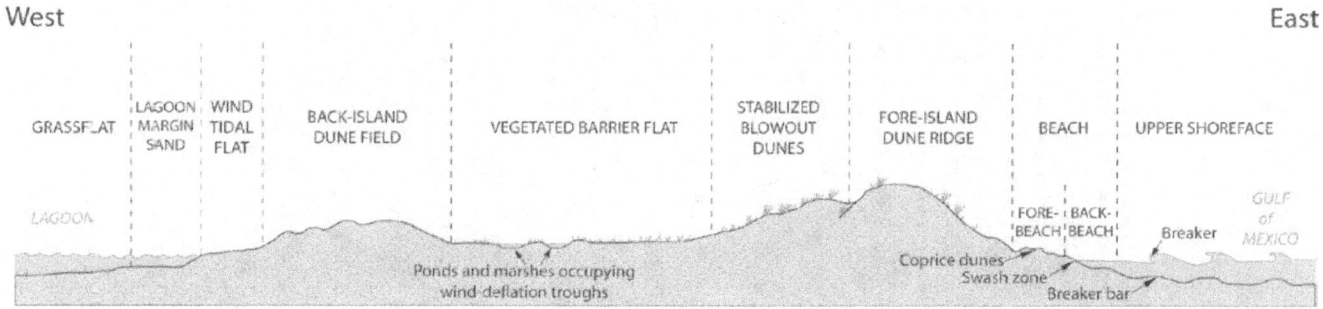

Figure 7. Geomorphic provinces at Padre Island National Seashore. Graphic redrafted from Weise and White (1980) by Trista Thornberry-Ehrlich (Colorado State University). Used with permission of the author and the University of Texas at Austin, Bureau of Economic Geology.

Figure 8. Beach and fore-island dune ridge. National Park Service photograph by Rebecca Beavers (NPS Geologic Resources Division).

Figure 9. Fore-island dune ridge. The fore-island dune ridge protects the barrier flats from storm impacts. National Park Service photograph available online 'http://www.nps.gov/pais/naturescience/Geology-Gallery.htm

Figure 10. Blowout. Blowouts occur where stabilizing vegetation has been lost or disturbed, resulting in the movement of sand. National Park Service photograph by Rebecca Beavers (NPS Geologic Resources Division).

Figure 11 Vegetated blow out dune. Vegetation stabilizes blow out dunes. National Park Service photograph available online http://www.nps.gov/pais/naturescience/Geology-Gallery.htm, accessed September 23, 2010.

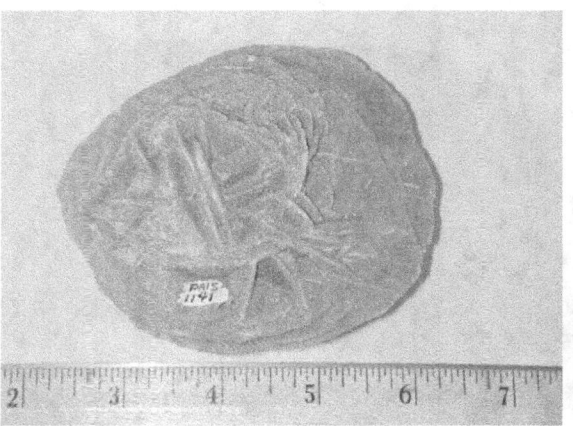 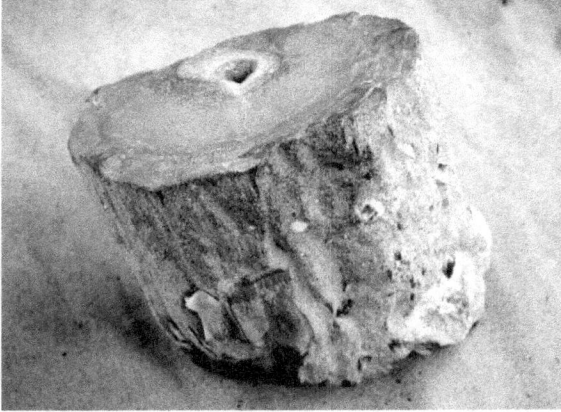

Figure 12. Sand rose and fulgurite. Rare gypsum rosettes (left) form in the Laguna Madre area, the only place in Texas where they occur. Ruler is in inches. Fulgurites (right) form when lightning strikes sand and fuses the grains together. Sometimes the center is completely "vaporized" leaving a hollow tube. National Park Service photographs available online: http://www.nps.gov/pais/naturescience/Geology.htm (accessed September 22, 2010).

Figure 13. Seashells of Padre Island. The wentletrap is one of the most sought-after shell along the Texas coast. Paper clip for scale. National Park Service graphic, available online: http://www.nps.gov/pais/photosmultimedia/Seashells.htm (accessed September 22, 2010).

Map Unit Properties

This section identifies characteristics of map units that appear on the Geologic Resources Inventory digital geologic map of Padre Island National Seashore. The accompanying table is highly generalized and for background purposes only. Ground-disturbing activities should not be permitted or denied on the basis of information in this table.

Geologic maps facilitate an understanding of Earth, its processes, and the geologic history responsible for its formation. Hence, the geologic map for Padre Island National Seashore provided information for the "Geologic Issues," "Geologic Features and Processes," and "Geologic History" sections of this report. Geologic maps are two-dimensional representations of complex three-dimensional relationships; their color coding illustrates the distribution of rocks and unconsolidated deposits. Bold lines that cross or separate the color patterns mark structures such as faults and folds. Point symbols indicate features such as dipping strata, sample localities, mines, wells, and cave openings.

Incorporation of geologic data into a Geographic Information System (GIS) increases the usefulness of geologic maps by revealing the spatial relationships among geologic features, other natural resources, and anthropogenic features. Geologic maps are indicators of water resources because they show which rock units are potential aquifers and are useful for finding seeps and springs. For example, on the digital geologic map for Padre Island National Seashore, unit B5 (sparsely vegetated barrier flat) has the greatest volume of freshwater of any map unit at Padre Island National Seashore. However, Boylan (1986) investigated the geohydrologic resources of the northern part of Padre Island and concluded that extensive withdrawal of groundwater from North Padre Island is not recommended because of the fragility of the ecosystems and dune forms.

Geologic maps are not soil maps, and do not show soil types, but they do show parent material—a key factor in soil formation. The following table incorporates information from *Soil Survey of Padre Island National Seashore, Texas* (Brezina 2004). Furthermore, resource managers have used geologic maps to make connections between geology and biology; for instance, geologic maps have served as tools for locating sensitive, threatened, and endangered plant species, which may prefer a particular map unit.

Although geologic maps do not show where earthquakes will occur, the presence of a fault indicates past movement and possible future seismic activity. Similarly, map units show areas that have been susceptible to hazards such as landslides, rockfalls, and volcanic eruptions. Geologic maps do not show archaeological or cultural resources, but past peoples may have inhabited or been influenced by depicted geomorphic features. For example, alluvial terraces may have been preferred use areas and formerly inhabited alcoves may occur at the contact between two rock units.

The geologic units listed in the following table correspond to the accompanying digital geologic data. Additionally, each map unit is part of a particular geomorphic environment (see "Geologic Features and Processes"). Map units cover barrier-island and lagoon environments, not marine environments, because mapping of offshore geology has not been completed (see "Benthic Habitat Mapping"). Map units are listed in the table from youngest to oldest. Geologically speaking, all the map units for Padre Island National Seashore are very young, hailing from the most recent geologic epoch—the Holocene (fig. 14). The table highlights characteristics of map units such as: susceptibility to erosion and hazards; the occurrence of paleontological resources (fossils), cultural resources, mineral resources, and caves or karst; and suitability as habitat or for recreational use. Some information on the table is conjectural and meant to serve as suggestions for further investigation.

The GRI digital geologic maps reproduce essential elements of the source maps including the unit descriptions, legend, map notes, graphics, and report. The following reference is the source for the GRI digital geologic data for Padre Island National Seashore:

Gibeaut, J., and T. Tremblay. 2005. Padre Island natural environments map (scale 1:5,000). Unpublished data. University of Texas, Bureau of Economic Geology, Austin, Texas, USA.

The GRI team implements a geology-GIS data model that standardizes map deliverables. This data model dictates GIS data structure including data layer architecture, feature attribution, and data relationships within ESRI ArcGIS software, and increases the overall utility of the data. GRI digital geologic map products include data in ESRI personal geodatabase and shapefile GIS formats, layer files with feature symbology, Federal Geographic Data Committee (FGDC)-compliant metadata, a Windows help file that contains all of the ancillary map information and graphics, and an ESRI ArcMap map document file that easily displays the map and connects the help file directly to the map document. GRI digital geologic data are included on the attached CD and are available through the NPS Data Store at http://science.nature.nps.gov/nrdata/. Data will be available on the Natural Resource Information Portal when the portal goes online. As of September 2010, access is limited to NPS computers at http://nrinfo/Home.mvc.

Map Unit Properties Table: Padre Island National Seashore

Age	Unit Name (Symbol)	Features and Description	Suitability for Infrastructure and Recreation	Hazards	Habitat
Man-made Units	Vegetated spoil mound (M1)	Partially vegetated, subaerial deposits of dredge material from the Gulf Intracoastal Waterway	Suitable for recreation but somewhat limited suitability for paths, trails, and 4WD trails. Very limited suitability for camp and picnic areas.	Flooding	Saline-water wetland plants and riparian shrubs, vines, and trees. Popular nesting grounds for a variety of bird species.
	Barren spoil mound (M2)	Barren, subaerial deposits of dredge material from the Gulf Intracoastal Waterway. Contains gypsum crystals.	Suitable for recreation but somewhat limited suitability for paths, trails, and 4WD trails. Very limited suitability for camp and picnic areas.	Flooding	Algal mats.
	Subaqueous spoil (M3)	Submerged dredge material from the Gulf Intracoastal Waterway	Unsuitable, submerged	None	Marine grass
	Modified land (M4)	Land modified by human activity	Disturbed by oil and gas exploration. Existing development.	Potential contamination from oil and gas spills or leaks	Alteration of natural environment evident on aerial photographs. Devegetation scars.
Barrier System Units	Beach (B1)	Sand and shell of varying compositions from north to south. Varying profile shapes and widths. Predominant internal structure (gently seaward-dipping planar laminations) produced by wave swash. *Mapping notes:* Bounded to the east by marine open waters of the Gulf of Mexico and landward by a prominent fore-island dune ridge. Gulfward shoreline captured from 2000 LIDAR data.	Tolerant of recreation but limited suitability for paths, trails, and 4WD trails. Very limited suitability for camp and picnic areas. Frequent wave surges and subsequent saltwater contamination.	Flooding	Foreshore is ecotone. Kemp's ridley turtle (*Lepidochelys kempi*) nesting site. Habitat for ghost crab (*Ocypode quadrata*), mole crab (*Emerita*), snails (*Olivella* and *Terebra*), staphylinid beetles, polychaete worm (*Lepidopa*), coquina clam (*Donax variabilis*), Texas pocket gopher (*Geomys personatus*) in backshore. Grasses. Freshwater and saline-water wetland plants in backbeach.
	Coppice dunes (B2)	Composed of fine beach sand. Characteristic mound appearance. Commonly found in backbeach, landward of fore-island dune ridge, and within sand flats. Forms broad fields where fore-island dune ridge is absent.	Unsuitable for development and recreation. Sensitive to vehicular and pedestrian traffic.	Blowing sand and migrating dunes	Animal species similar to beach habitat
	Fore-island dune ridge (B3)	Grass-covered or sparsely vegetated. Fine, well-sorted sand containing rare shells. Parallels the Gulf of Mexico shoreline, becoming less prominent farther south on the island. *Mapping notes:* Vegetated surfaces interpreted primarily from 2003 photographs. Boundary frequently interpreted through comparison with 2000 LIDAR DEM. Aerial photography signature alone did not provide sufficient information to delineate dune extent; however, the high vertical resolution of the LIDAR allowed delineation of the dune ridge throughout the entire length of the island.	Unsuitable for development and recreation and recreation should not be breached. Lens of fresh groundwater underneath, thinning towards back-island dune system.	Inundation and erosion during hurricanes. First landward defense against floods and storms.	Plants zoned by elevation on the dunes. Lower: marsh hay cordgrass (*Spartina patens*), morning glory (*Ipomoea* spp.), and sea purslane (*Sesuvium portulacastrum*). Middle and upper: sea oats (*Uniola paniculata*), bitter panicum (*Panicum amarum*), and gulf croton (*Croton punctatus*). Backside of foredunes: seacoast bluestem (*Andropogon scoparius littoralis*). Ghost crab, burrowing mammals, and reptiles
	Vegetated barrier flat (B4)	Most common terrestrial environment. Fine and coarse sand and shells. Includes heavily vegetated stabilized dunes. Located behind fore-island dune ridge.	Remains of three (ranching) line camps. Suitable for recreation but very limited suitability for paths, trails, 4WD trails, and camp and picnic areas. Groundwater withdrawal and water diversion could easily kill vegetation, resulting in dune migration.	Flooding and ponding	Grasses. Riparian shrubs, vines, and trees. Freshwater wetland plants. Pocket gophers, moles, weasels, ground squirrels, mice, and snakes; occasionally coyotes, shrews, bats, raccoons, skunks, rats, jackrabbits, and armadillos. Insects abound.
	Temporarily flooded brackish to fresh marsh (B4a)	Forms in deeper, troughlike wind-deflation flats. Floored by mostly sand, also mud and plant debris. *Mapping notes:* Lightest tone of marsh signatures. Visible on 2005 photographs but absent on 2002 and 1995 photographs.	Sensitive to recreation	Flooding and ponding	Various forms of algae. Plants such as common cattail (*Typha domingensis*), American bulrush (*Scirpus americanus*), in marshy areas.
	Salt marsh (B4b)	Forms in deeper, troughlike wind-deflation flats. Floored by mostly sand, also mud and plant debris. *Mapping notes:* Characteristic dark signature adjacent to saltwater bodies or areas frequently flooded with saltwater. Undivided.	Sensitive to recreation	Flooding and ponding	Shoregrass (*Monanthochloe littoralis*), inland saltgrass (*Distichlis spicata*), bushy sea-oxeye (*Borrichia frutescens*), and perennial forbs
	Seasonally flooded brackish to fresh marsh (B4c)	Forms in deeper, troughlike wind-deflation flats. Floored by mostly sand, also mud and plant debris. *Mapping notes:* Visible on 2003 and 2002 photographs. Mostly absent from 1995 photographs.	Sensitive to recreation	Flooding and ponding	Various forms of algae. Plants such as common cattail (*Typha domingensis*), American bulrush (*Scirpus americanus*), and spikerushes (*Eleocharis* sp.) in marshy areas.
	Semipermanently flooded brackish to fresh marsh (B4d)	Forms in deeper, troughlike wind-deflation flats. Floored by mostly sand, also mud and plant debris. *Mapping notes:* Darkest marsh signature. Visible on all vintages of photographs.	Sensitive to recreation	Flooding and ponding	Various forms of algae. Plants such as common cattail (*Typha domingensis*), American bulrush (*Scirpus americanus*), and spikerushes (*Eleocharis* sp.) in marshy areas.
	Sparsely vegetated barrier flat (B5)	Highly fragmented vegetation. Barren areas expose oldest sand in the national seashore.	Suitable water source for groundwater withdrawal. Greatest volume of freshwater of any map unit.	Flooding and ponding. Active blowout dunes.	Potential habitat for grasses. Riparian shrubs, vines, and trees. Freshwater wetland plants. Pocket gophers, moles, weasels, ground squirrels, mice, and snakes; occasionally coyotes, shrews, bats, raccoons, skunks, ants, jackrabbits, and armadillos.

Age for Barrier System Units: QUATERNARY (Holocene Epoch)

Age	Unit Name (Symbol)	Features and Description	Suitability for Infrastructure and Recreation	Hazards	Habitat
QUATERNARY (Holocene Epoch) — Barrier Island Units	Stabilized dune (B5a)	Moderately vegetated blowout dunes in elongate or parabolic forms. Sediment derived from fore-island dune ridge. *Mapping notes:* Distinct from vegetated barrier flat through sharp and bright signature of underlying dune sand.	Unsuitable for development and recreation. Should not be disturbed.	Second defense against floods and storms	Grasses such as bitter panicum (*Panicum amarum*), bitter panicum (*Panicum amarum*), gulfdune paspalum (*Paspalum vaginatum*), and diuspeed (*Sporobolus silveanus*)
	Storm washover channel (B7)	Non-vegetated conduit as much as 213 m (700 ft) wide for sand, shells, and water during storms. Mud in ponded areas. *Mapping notes:* Found exclusively in the southern third of the map area (South Padre Island).	Unsuitable for developments. Hurricane-formed feature. Cuts through fore-island dune ridges.	Inundation during hurricanes. Ponding.	Algal mats around edges of ponds
	Storm washover fan (B7a)	Non-vegetated sand deposit from washover channel. Slight topographic relief on gulfward end but grades imperceptibly into back-island environments.	Unsuitable for developments. Hurricane deposit.	Inundation during hurricanes	Non-vegetated
	Wind-deflation flat (B8)	Sand and finer sediments with shell and cobble lag deposit. Mud drapes. Transitional between barrier and lagoon environments. *Mapping notes:* Found in southern third of the map area (South Padre Island).	Unsuitable for development. Serves as storm-water runway.	Storm waters deposit sediment on unit. Flooding and ponding in troughs.	Algal mats
	Sand flat (B8a)	Non-vegetated, high sand flat. Commonly fringing back-island vegetated barrier flats and coppice dunes.	Unsuitable for development	Blowing sand and rapidly migrating dunes. Flooding.	Non-vegetated
	Water (B9)	Larger ponds and marshes. Ephemeral. Forms in deeper troughs of wind-deflation flats.	Ponds serve as discharge areas during fall and spring (wet seasons) and recharge areas during summer and winter (dry seasons) of groundwater system.	Ponds contain pathogenic organisms. Should not be used for potable water.	Various forms of algae. Plants such as common cattail (*Typha domingensis*), American bulrush (*Scirpus americanus*), and spikerushes (*Eleocharis* sp.) in marshy areas.
	Dredged channel (B9a)	Gulf Intracoastal Waterway and Mansfield Channel. Contains gypsum crystals.	Suitable for boating and fishing. Maintenance dredging required to keep channels open. Laguna Madre sensitive to changing salinity and hydrological conditions.	Sedimentation, turbidity, and resuspension of contaminants	Negative impacts to grass flats, vertebrate and invertebrate marine species, and nesting-bird habitat.
	Active dunes (B10)	Devegetated. Fine sands. Back-island dune field and fore-island blowout dunes. Exemplifies barrier-island migration toward the Texas mainland. *Mapping notes:* Bright, nearly white signature on photographs.	Unsuitable for development and recreation. Should not be breached.	Blowing sand and migrating dunes	Burrowing mammals and reptiles
	Back-island sand flat (B11)	Non-vegetated, small migrating dunes. Transitional from back-island dune field to wind-tidal flat.	Unsuitable for development and recreation. Sensitive to vehicular and pedestrian traffic.	Rapid changes in dune forms. Flooding.	Algal mats. Texas pocket gopher.
Lagoon System Units	Wind-tidal flat with small dunes (L1)	Loose wind-blown sand. Contains gypsum crystals. Forms in Land-Cut area.	Unsuitable for development and recreation. Highly susceptible to vehicular and pedestrian traffic. Cut by Gulf Intracoastal Waterway. Brine (hypersaline) groundwater.	Inundation during hurricanes. Migrating dunes. Rarely flooded by wind tides.	Saline-water wetland plants. Macroinvertebrates. Piping plover. Texas pocket gopher.
	Wind-tidal flat with firm sand and mud (L2)	Higher areas rarely flooded. Lagoonward fringes of back-island area.	Unsuitable for development and recreation. Highly susceptible to vehicular and pedestrian traffic. Cut by Gulf Intracoastal Waterway. Brine (hypersaline) groundwater.	Inundation during hurricanes. Rarely flooded by wind tides.	Saline-water wetland plants. Macroinvertebrates. Piping plover.
	Wind-tidal flat with algal mats (L3)	Sand and mud. Alternately emergent/submergent.	Unsuitable. Highly susceptible to vehicular and pedestrian traffic. Cut by Gulf Intracoastal Waterway. Brine (hypersaline) groundwater.	Inundation during hurricanes. Frequent flooding. Ponding.	Algal mats. Saline-water wetland plants. macroinvertebrates. Piping plover.
	Vegetated sand and shell berms (L4)	Vegetated, accretionary, subaerial, natural islands (i.e., North Bird and South Bird islands)	Development and recreation prohibited. Wildlife sanctuary.	Storm waves	Bitter panicgrass (*Panicum amarum*), perennial forbs, sea oats (*Uniola paniculata*), camphorweed (*Pluchea Cass.*), and seacoast bluestem (*Schizachyrium scoparium*). Popular nesting grounds for a variety of bird species.
	Lagoon-margin sand (L5)	Subaqueous to emergent, usually submerged under as much as 0.9 m (3 ft) of water. Sand waves and ripples common.	Unsuitable. Generally submerged.	Flooding and ponding	High-energy lagoon margin. Typically unvegetated.
	Grassflat (L6)	Mud including shell and grass. Generally covered by <1.2 m (4 ft) of water. Shallowest parts exposed at low tide.	Unsuitable. Submerged. High biologic productivity easily disturbed by changes in turbidity, salinity, and water depth.	None	Algae. Marine grasses, primarily shoalgrass (*Halodule wrightii*), also widgeon grass (*Ruppia maritima*), turtlegrass (*Thalassia testudinum*), clovergrass (*Halophila engelmannii*), and manateegrass (*Cymodocea manatorum*). Saline-water wetland plants. Extensive invertebrate population. Breeding grounds for fish and waterbird species.

Geologic History

This section describes the rocks and unconsolidated deposits that appear on the digital geologic map of Padre Island National Seashore the environment in which those units were deposited, and the timing of geologic events that created the present landscape.

Along the gently sloping continental shelf of eastern Texas, near the Rio Grande, Colorado River, and Brazos River deltas, many factors converged to favor barrier-island development, namely an ample sediment supply and waves that break far from the shoreline. Add to this a change between regressive and transgressive conditions (table 4), and Padre Island literally took shape.

Between 125,000 and 110,000 years ago, the continental shelf built up as rivers deposited deltaic mud and fluvial sand (Beaumont Formation) during the Sangamon interglacial stage (Morton and Price 1987). The Sangamon was the "warm period" between the Illinoian and Wisconsinan glaciations. The Wisconsinan was the last major advance of continental-scale glaciers on North America. Strand-plain deposits (sand reworked by waves and currents at the prograded shoreline) marked the seaward extent of delta advance (Morton and McGowen 1980). About 50,000 years ago, sea level dropped during a regression (table 4). Rivers eroded the fluvial-deltaic deposits on the exposed continental shelf, creating a network of deep valleys. Depths of these valleys range from 15 m to 38 m (50 ft to 125 ft) below present-day sea level (Fisk 1959).

Approximately 18,000 years ago, sea level began to rise rapidly, flooding the entrenched river valleys. Estuaries formed in the lower valleys, and the upper valleys filled with fluvial-deltaic deposits. Large rivers with large watersheds (e.g., the Rio Grande and Brazos River) carried enough sediment to fill their valleys and build deltas into the Gulf of Mexico. The unfilled, former river valleys became today's major bays (e.g., Galveston, Mobile, and Pensacola) (Morton 1994).

Rapid sea level rise (transgression) persisted until about 4,500 years ago when the rate of sea-level rise slowed. Barrier islands began forming, initially as submerged shoals on drainage divides (topographic highs) between the river valleys that cut into the continental shelf. Erosion of Pleistocene (2.6 million to 11,700 years old) strand-plain sand supplied sediment for barrier-island development (Morton and McGowen 1980). The shoals became a series of discontinuous, sandy islands (Morton and McGowen 1980). About 3,700 years ago, these small islands coalesced into a continuous barrier that ran parallel to the mainland. This barrier enclosed Laguna Madre.

As hurricanes and prevailing southeasterly winds transported sand across the island, a deeper, open lagoonal system evolved into a shallow, closed hypersaline system. The width of Laguna Madre decreased, and finer sediments accumulated in the center (Morton and McGowen 1980). Fisk (1959) estimated that about 170 years ago central Laguna Madre became filled with sand derived from Padre Island. The fill, which is characteristic of the Land Cut, divided Laguna Madre into a northern and southern section. Laguna Madre will eventually become filled from the Land Cut northward to Baffin Bay (Morton and McGowen 1980).

Since their inception, various parts of the barrier chain have (1) prograded seaward by the deposition of sand on their shorefaces, (2) remained stationary (aggraded), or (3) moved landward by shoreface erosion (retrograded). Aggradational barriers occupy the same general geographic position and grow vertically in response to abundant sediment supply and a relative rise in sea level, rather than growing seaward as do progradational barriers (Morton 1994). Progradational and aggradational barriers are wide, thick, and have high topographic profiles that effectively prevent storm surges from washing over the islands (Morton 1994). Retrogradational barriers are narrow, thin, and have low topographic profiles that allow repeated overwash by even minor storm surges (Morton 1994).

Two of these geomorphic modes are apparent at Padre Island National Seashore. The northern and central segments of the national seashore have remained stationary and grown upward as an aggradational barrier (fig. 15). The southern (retrogradational) part has migrated lagoonward.

Both progradational and aggradational barrier types began as retrogradational, but the availability of sand from the converging Brazos-Colorado and Rio Grande deltas allowed the central and northern parts of Padre Island National Seashore to become aggradational (Morton 1994). The shoreline curvature (concave seaward), predominant wind directions, and deficit in annual rainfall also contributed to development of an aggradational barrier. Eolian processes prevent progradation, that is, significant seaward migration and loss of sand from the beach. Under relatively stable sea-level conditions, this central segment of the barrier island continues to aggrade as windblown sand is transported onto the barrier and stored on it (Morton 1994).

The southern part of Padre Island National Seashore is a retrogradational barrier (fig. 15). Such barriers typically form along shoreline segments that are either straight or convex seaward. This configuration focuses wave energy and promotes sediment transport away from the barrier, leaving it starved for sand (Morton 1994).

Retrogradational barriers are also known as "transgressive" or "low-profile" barriers. The southern retrogradational barrier of the national seashore originated from, and is located at, the retreating flank of the Rio Grande delta. The diagnostic feature of this type of island is the sharp contact of the sand with the underlying lagoonal sediments (Dickinson et al. 1972). At Padre Island National Seashore, the modern barrier island is a thin wedge of sand situated over Holocene and Pleistocene mud of the founding Rio Grande delta (Morton 1994). Presently, little sand is available for maintenance of South Padre Island because of dams on the Rio Grande and jetties at Brazos Santiago Pass (Morton 1994).

Texas barriers are entering a new phase of their evolution as a result of recent decreases in sediment supply and increases in the rate of relative sea-level rise (Morton 1994). Erosion of both the Gulf of Mexico and Laguna Madre shorelines is causing most barriers to narrow. Moreover, retrogradational barriers, including the southern part of Padre Island National Seashore, are continuing to migrate landward. Central Padre Island, including the central and northern parts of Padre Island National Seashore, is an exception among the Texas barriers; it remains an actively aggrading island as a result of converging littoral currents. The sediment supplied to the beaches, dunes, and wind-tidal flats of this part of Padre Island is sufficient to maintain a stable landform even as relative sea level is rising (Morton 1994).

Table 4. Transgressive and regressive characteristics of shorelines

Transgression	Regression
Interglacial stage	Glacial stage
High (or rising) sea level	Low (or decreasing) sea level
Warmer climatic conditions	Colder climatic conditions
Low (or decreasing) precipitation	Abundant (or increasing) precipitation
Low (or decreasing) sediment supply	Abundant (or increasing) sediment supply
Decreasing streamflow	Increasing streamflow
Fluvial valley aggradation or non-erosion	Fluvial valley entrenchment or erosion
Shoreface retreat (landward)	Shoreface progradation and advance (seaward)
Delta retreat (landward)	Delta progradation and advance (seaward)
Sediments thickening landward (updip)	Sediments thickening seaward (downdip)
Barrier-lagoon formation	Strand-plain formation

Eon	Era	Period	Epoch	Ma	Life Forms	North American Events
Phanerozoic	Cenozoic	Quaternary	Holocene	0.01	Modern humans	Cascade volcanoes (W)
			Pleistocene		Extinction of large mammals and birds	Worldwide glaciation
				2.6		
		Tertiary / Neogene	Pliocene		Large carnivores	Sierra Nevada Mountains (W)
			Miocene	5.3	Whales and apes	Linking of North and South America
				23.0		Basin-and-Range extension (W)
		Tertiary / Paleogene	Oligocene	33.9		
			Eocene	55.8	Early primates	Laramide Orogeny ends (W)
			Paleocene			
		65.5				
	Mesozoic	Cretaceous			Mass extinction	Laramide Orogeny (W)
					Placental mammals	Sevier Orogeny (W)
				145.5	Early flowering plants	Nevadan Orogeny (W)
		Jurassic			First mammals	Elko Orogeny (W)
				199.6	Mass extinction	Breakup of Pangaea begins
		Triassic			Flying reptiles	Sonoma Orogeny (W)
					First dinosaurs	
		251				
	Paleozoic	Permian			Mass extinction	Supercontinent Pangaea intact
					Coal-forming forests diminish	Ouachita Orogeny (S)
						Alleghanian (Appalachian) Orogeny (E)
				299		Ancestral Rocky Mountains (W)
		Pennsylvanian			Coal-forming swamps	
					Sharks abundant	
				318.1	Variety of insects	
		Mississippian			First amphibians	
				359.2	First reptiles	Antler Orogeny (W)
		Devonian			Mass extinction	
					First forests (evergreens)	Acadian Orogeny (E-NE)
				416		
		Silurian			First land plants	
				443.7	Mass extinction	
		Ordovician			First primitive fish	
					Trilobite maximum	Taconic Orogeny (E-NE)
					Rise of corals	
				488.3		
		Cambrian				Avalonian Orogeny (NE)
					Early shelled organisms	Extensive oceans cover most of proto-North America (Laurentia)
		542				
Proterozoic		Precambrian			First multicelled organisms	Supercontinent rifted apart / Formation of early supercontinent
						Grenville Orogeny (E)
					Jellyfish fossil (670 Ma)	First iron deposits / Abundant carbonate rocks
				2500		
Archean					Early bacteria and algae	
				≈4000		Oldest known Earth rocks (≈3.96 billion years ago)
Hadean					Origin of life?	Oldest moon rocks (4–4.6 billion years ago)
						Formation of Earth's crust
		4600			Formation of the Earth	

Age of Mammals (Cenozoic life forms); *Age of Dinosaurs* (Mesozoic); *Age of Amphibians*, *Fishes*, *Marine Invertebrates* (Paleozoic).

Figure 14. Geologic timescale. Included are major life history and tectonic events occurring on the North American continent. Red lines indicate major unconformities between eras. Radiometric ages shown are in millions of years (Ma). Compass directions in parentheses indicate the regional location of individual geologic events. Adapted from the U.S. Geological Survey, http://pubs.usgs.gov/fs/2007/3015/ with additional information from the International Commission on Stratigraphy. http://www.stratigraphy.org/view.php?id=25.

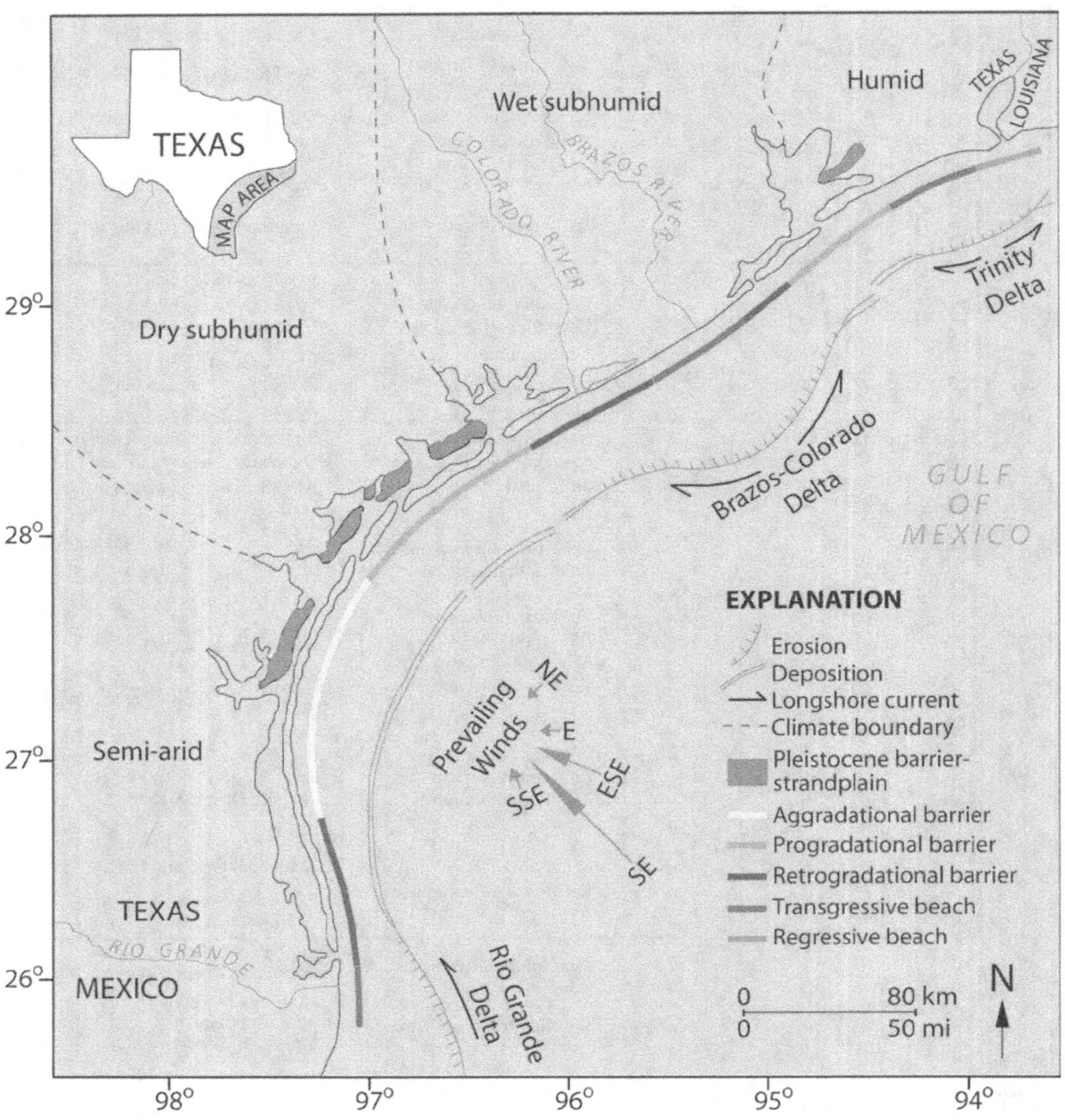

Figure 15. Barrier island morphology. Barriers vary as a result of climate, shoreline geometry, patterns of longshore drift, past changes in sea-level rise, and sediment supply. Padre Island National Seashore is primarily an aggradational barrier, but the southern part is a retrogradational barrier. Graphic redrafted after Morton (1994) by Trista Thornberry-Ehrlich (Colorado State University).

Glossary

This glossary contains brief definitions of technical geologic terms used in this report. Not all geologic terms used are referenced. For more detailed definitions or to find terms not listed here please visit: http://geomaps.wr.usgs.gov/parks/misc/glossarya.html. Definitions are based on those in the American Geological Institute Glossary of Geology (fifth edition; 2005).

amphibole. A common group of rock-forming silicate minerals. Hornblende is the most abundant type.

aquifer. A rock or sedimentary unit that is sufficiently porous that it has a capacity to hold water, sufficiently permeable to allow water to move through it, and currently saturated to some level.

astronomical tide. Also called "equilibrium tide." A hypothetical global form of the sea-surface elevation which would be in equilibrium with the lunar and solar tide-generating forces in the absence of inertia and currents, and no continents.

barchan dune. A crescent-shaped dune with arms or horns of the crescent pointing downwind. The crescent or barchan type is most characteristic of inland desert regions.

barrier island. A long, low, narrow island formed by a ridge of sand that parallels the coast.

beach. A gently sloping shoreline covered with sediment, commonly formed by the action of waves and tides.

beach face. The section of the beach exposed to direct wave and/or tidal action.

bed. The smallest sedimentary strata unit, commonly ranging in thickness from one centimeter to a meter or two and distinguishable from beds above and below.

bedding. Depositional layering or stratification of sediments.

blowout. A geomorphology term for a small saucer-, cup-, or trough-shaped hollow or depression formed by wind erosion on a preexisting dune or other sand deposit. Commonly applies to areas of shifting sand or loose soil, where vegetation is disturbed or destroyed. Generally includes the adjoining accumulation of sand derived from the depression. Some blowouts maybe many kilometers in diameter.

biotite. A widely distributed and important rock-forming mineral of the mica group. Forms thin, flat sheets.

carbonate. A mineral that has CO_3^{-2} as its essential component (e.g., calcite and aragonite).

carbonate rock. A rock consisting chiefly of carbonate minerals (e.g., limestone, dolomite, or carbonatite).

clastic. Describes rock or sediment made of fragments of pre-existing rocks (clasts).

clay. Can be used to refer to clay minerals or as a sedimentary fragment size classification (less than 1/256 mm [0.00015 in]).

claystone. Lithified clay having the texture and composition of shale but lacking shale's fine layering and fissility (characteristic splitting into thin layers).

continental shelf. The shallowly submerged part of a continental margin extending from the shoreline to the continental slope with water depths less than 200 m (660 ft).

coppice dune. Also called "shrub-coppice dune," "coppice mound," or "nebkha." A small, streamlined dune that forms to the lee of bush-and-clump vegetation on a smooth surface of very shallow sand.

coquina. Limestone composed of cemented shell fragments.

cross bedding. Uniform to highly varied sets of inclined sedimentary beds ("cross beds") deposited by wind or water that indicate flow conditions such as water flow direction and depth.

cross section. A graphical interpretation of geology, structure, and/or stratigraphy in the third (vertical) dimension based on mapped and measured geological extents and attitudes depicted in a vertically oriented plane.

cross stratum. A cross bed.

delta. A sediment wedge deposited where a stream flows into a lake or sea.

dip. The angle between a bed or other geologic surface and horizontal.

dune. A low mound or ridge of sediment, usually sand, deposited by wind. Common dune types include "barchan," "longitudinal," "parabolic," and "transverse" (see respective listings).

eolian. Describes materials formed, eroded, or deposited by or related to the action of the wind. Also spelled "Aeolian."

estuary. The seaward end or tidal mouth of a river where freshwater and seawater mix; many estuaries are drowned river valleys caused by sea-level rise (transgression) or coastal subsidence.

eustatic. Relates to simultaneous worldwide rise or fall of sea level.

evaporite. A sedimentary rock composed primarily of minerals produced from a saline solution as a result of extensive or total evaporation of the solvent (usually water).

feldspar. A group of abundant (more than 60% of Earth's crust), light-colored to translucent silicate minerals found in all types of rocks. Usually white and gray to pink. May contain potassium, sodium, calcium, barium, rubidium, and strontium along with aluminum, silica, and oxygen.

formation. Fundamental rock-stratigraphic unit that is mappable, lithologically distinct from adjoining strata, and has definable upper and lower contacts.

garnet. A hard mineral that has a glassy luster, often with well defined crystal faces, and a variety of colors, dark red being characteristic. Commonly found in metamorphic rocks.

glauconite. A green mineral, closely related to the micas. It is an indicator of very slow sedimentation.

hornblende. The most common mineral of the amphibole group. Hornblende is commonly black and occurs in distinct crystals or in columnar, fibrous, or granular forms.

igneous. Refers to a rock or mineral that originated from molten material; one of the three main classes of rocks—igneous, metamorphic, and sedimentary.

Interglacial stage. A subdivision of a glacial epoch separating two glaciations. Characterized by a relatively long period of warm or mild climate during which temperature rose to at least that of the present day; especially an interval of the Pleistocene Epoch, as the "Sangamon Interglacial Stage."

lamination. Very thin, parallel layers.

longitudinal dune. Dune elongated parallel to the direction of wind flow.

longshore current. A current parallel to a coastline caused by waves approaching the shore at an oblique angle.

marl. An unconsolidated deposit commonly with shell fragments and sometimes glauconite consisting chiefly of clay and calcium carbonate that formed under marine or freshwater conditions.

metamorphic. Describes the process of metamorphism or its results. One of the three main classes of rocks—igneous, metamorphic, and sedimentary.

metamorphism. Literally, a change in form. Metamorphism occurs in rocks through mineral alteration, formation, and/or recrystallization from increased heat and/or pressure.

mineral. A naturally occurring, inorganic crystalline solid with a definite chemical composition or compositional range.

mud cracks. Cracks formed in clay, silt, or mud by shrinkage during dehydration at Earth's surface.

parabolic dune. Crescent-shaped dune with horns or arms that point upwind.

progradation. The seaward building of land area due to sedimentary deposition.

pyroxene. A common rock-forming mineral. It is characterized by short, stout crystals.

regression. A long-term seaward retreat of the shoreline or relative fall of sea level.

ripple. The undulating, approximately parallel and usually small-scale ridge pattern formed on sediment by the flow of wind or water.

rock. A solid, cohesive aggregate of one or more minerals.

rutile. A reddish brown titanium oxide mineral. It occurs as a primary mineral in some igneous rocks, in metamorphic rocks, and as residual grains in beach sands.

Saffir-Simpson hurricane intensity scale. A five-category hurricane intensity scale developed by H. S. Saffir and R. H. Simpson that rates hurricanes from 1 to 5 on the basis of maximum sustained wind speed. Categories are 1 (weak), 2 (moderate), 3 (strong), 4 (very strong), and 5 (devastating).

sand. A clastic particle smaller than a granule and larger than a silt grain, having a diameter in the range of 1/16 mm (0.0025 in) to 2 mm (0.08 in).

sandstone. Clastic sedimentary rock of predominantly sand-sized grains.

scour and fill. A sedimentary structure consisting of a small erosional channel, generally ellipsoidal, that is subsequently filled; a small-scale washout.

sediment. An eroded and deposited, unconsolidated accumulation of rock and mineral fragments.

sedimentary rock. A consolidated and lithified rock consisting of clastic and/or chemical sediment(s). One of the three main classes of rocks—igneous, metamorphic, and sedimentary.

serpulid. A round, segmented ocean worm of the Family Serpulidae with a crown of tentacles and a flat coiled shell.

silt. Clastic sedimentary material intermediate in size between fine-grained sand and coarse clay (1/256 to 1/16 mm [0.00015 to 0.002 in]).

slope. The inclined surface of any geomorphic feature or measurement thereof. Synonymous with "gradient."

soil. Surface accumulation of weathered rock and organic matter capable of supporting plant growth and often overlying the parent material from which it formed.

staurolite. A dark reddish-brown, blackish-brown, yellowish-brown, or blue mineral. Twinned crystals often resemble a cross. It is a common constituent of rocks such as mica schist and gneiss that have undergone metamorphism. Also called: staurotide, cross-stone, grenatite, and fairy stone.

strand plain. A shore built seaward by waves and currents and continuous for some distance along the coast.

strata. Tabular or sheet-like masses or distinct layers of rock.

stratigraphy. The geologic study of the origin, occurrence, distribution, classification, correlation, and age of rock layers, especially sedimentary rocks.

swash. The rush of water up the beach face after a wave has broken.

tourmaline. A crystal silicate mineral occurring in three-, six-, or nine-sided prisms composed of elements such as sodium, calcium, magnesium, iron, aluminum, lithium, and sometime fluorine in small amounts. Tourmaline is classed as a semi-precious stone and the gem comes in a wide variety of colors.

transgression. Landward migration of the sea as a result of a relative rise in sea level.

transverse dune. Dune elongated perpendicular to the prevailing wind direction. The leeward slope stands at or near the angle of repose of sand whereas the windward slope is comparatively gentle.

water table. The upper surface of the saturated zone; the zone of rock in an aquifer saturated with water.

zircon. A common accessory mineral in siliceous igneous rocks, crystalline limestone, schist, and gneiss, also in sedimentary rocks derived from and in beach and river placer deposits. When cut and polished, the colorless varieties provide exceptionally brilliant gemstones. Very durable mineral, often used for age-dating.

Literature Cited

This section lists references cited in this report. A more complete geologic bibliography is available from the National Park Service Geologic Resources Division.

Andrews, J. 1972. Shell collecting in the Padre Island National Seashore. Pages 31–35 *in* R. F. Travis, R. N. Tench, W. D. Hodgson, D. C. Callaway, and H. Wyneken, editors. Padre Island National Seashore Field Guide. GCAGS Convention Field Trip, October 14, 1972. Gulf Coast Association of Geological Societies, Corpus Christi, Texas, USA.

Babcock & Brown. 2008. Harvesting the wind of the South Texas gulf coast. Online presentation. Babcock & Brown, Sydney, Australia. http://www.kenedy.org/KenedyRanch/tabid/1093/Default.aspx (accessed September 1, 2010).

Baccus, J. T., and J. K. Horton. 1979. An ecological and sedimentary study of Padre Island National Seashore. Southwest Texas State University, San Marco, Texas, USA.

Baccus, J. T., and J. K. Horton. 1982. Pedestrian impacts: Padre Island. Pages 89–102 *in* B. Mayo and L. Smith, editors. Proceedings of Barrier Island Forum and Workshop, Provincetown, Massachusetts, May 28–30, 1980. National Park Service, North Atlantic Region, Boston, Massachusetts, USA.

Baccus, J. T., J. K. Horton, and P. D. Carangelo. 1977. A study of beach and dunes floral and faunal interrelations as influenced by recreational and user impact on Padre Island National Seashore. Southwest Texas State University, San Marcos, Texas, USA.

Barajas, M. 2010. South Padre Island largely unscathed by Hurricane Alex. Online news article. The Monitor (2010-07-01 20:06:09). Freedom Communications, Inc., Irvine, California, USA. http://www.themonitor.com/common/printer/view.php?db=monitortx&id=40402 (accessed August 31, 2010).

Beavers, R. 2005. Sea-level impacts to coastal parks. Page 31 *in* J. Selleck, editor. Natural Resource Year in Review—2004. Technical Information Center (TIC) publication number D-1609. U.S. Department of the Interior, National Park Service, Natural Resource Information Division, Denver, Colorado, USA.

Behrens, E. W., P. D. Carangelo, and H. S. Finkelstein. 1976. Effect of vehicular and pedestrian traffic on backshore vegetation and beach development, beach impact study, Padre Island National Seashore. Final report for contract CX700050448. National Park Service, Southwest Regional Office, Santa Fe, New Mexico, USA.

Behrens, E. W., R. L. Watson, P. D. Carangelo, W. H. Sohl, and H. S. Finkelstein. 1975. Effect of vehicular and pedestrian traffic on backshore vegetation and dune development, beach impact study, Padre Island National Seashore. Final report for contract CX700040146. Technical Information Center (TIC) publication number D-88. National Park Service, Southwest Regional Office, Santa Fe, New Mexico, USA.

Blum, M., and J. R. Jones. 1985. Variation in vegetation density and foredune complexity at North Padre Island, Texas. Texas Journal of Science 37:63–73.

Boker, T. A. 1953. Sand dunes on northern Padre Island, Texas. Thesis. University of Kansas, Lawrence, Kansas, USA.

Boylan, D. M. 1986. The hydrologic resources of North Padre Island, coastal South Texas. Thesis. Baylor University, Waco, Texas, USA.

Breuer, J. P. 1957. An ecological survey of Baffin and Alazan bays, Texas. Publications of the Institute of Marine Science 4(2):134–155.

Brezina, D. N. 2004. Soil survey of Padre Island National Seashore, Texas, special report. Natural Resources Conservation Service, National Park Service, and Texas Agricultural Experiment Station, Washington, D.C., USA.

Brown, L. F., J. L. Brewton, T. J. Evans, J. H. McGowen, W. A. White, W. L. Fisher, and C. G. Groat. 1976. Environmental geologic atlas of the Texas coastal zone: Corpus Christi area. University of Texas, Bureau of Economic Geology, Austin, Texas, USA.

Brown, L. F., J. L. Brewton, T. J. Evans, J. H. McGowen, W. A. White, C. G. Groat, and W. L. Fisher. 1977. Environmental geologic atlas of the Texas coastal zone: Kingsville area. University of Texas, Bureau of Economic Geology, Austin, Texas, USA.

Brown, L. F., J. L. Brewton, T. J. Evans, J. H. McGowen, W. A. White, C. G. Groat, and W. L. Fisher. 1980. Environmental geologic atlas of the Texas coastal zone: Brownsville-Harlingen area. University of Texas, Bureau of Economic Geology, Austin, Texas, USA.

Bullard, F. M. 1942. Source of beach and river sands on gulf coast of Texas. Geological Society of America Bulletin 53(7):1021–1043.

Callaway, B. 1972. History of Padre Island. Pages 28–30 in R. F. Travis, R. N. Tench, W. D. Hodgson, D. C.

Callaway, and H. Wyneken, editors. Padre Island National Seashore Field Guide, GCAGS Convention Field Trip, October 14, 1972. Gulf Coast Association of Geological Societies, Corpus Christi, Texas, USA.

Chaney, A. H., B. R. Chapman, J. P. Karges, D. A. Nelson, and R. R. Schmit. 1978. Use of dredged material islands by colonial seabirds and wading birds in Texas. Texas A&I University, Kingsville, Texas, USA.

Christensen, B. 2009. Port Mansfield Channel navigable once again. Online news article. The Monitor (April 11, 2009). http://www.themonitor.com/articles/channel-25295-mansfield-wilson.html (accessed September 1, 2010).

Cochran, S. A., A. E. Gibbs, and J. B. Logan. 2007. Geologic resource evaluation of Pu'uhonua O Hōnaunau National Historical Park, Hawai'i: Part II—Benthic habitat mapping. Scientific Investigations Report 2006-5258. U.S. Geological Survey, Reston, Virginia, USA.

Conti, R. 2007. When dunes walk over dune walkovers. Gulf Coast Association of Geological Societies Transactions 57:151–163.

Dansby, L., D. Echols, and E. Martinez. 2008. Benthic invertebrate diversity and density on the Gulf of Mexico beach, Padre Island National Seashore, October 30, 2008. Draft funding proposal for Youth Partnership Program (YPP). National Park Service, Intermountain Regional Office; Padre Island National Seashore; and New Mexico Highlands University; Santa Fe, New Mexico; Corpus Christi, Texas; and Las Vegas, New Mexico, USA.

Dickinson, K. A., H. L. Berryhill, Jr., and C. W. Holmes. 1972. Criteria for recognizing ancient barrier coastlines. Pages 192–214 in J. K. Rigby and W. K. Hamblin, editors. Recognition of ancient barrier environments. Special Publication 16. Society of Economic Paleontologists and Mineralogists (SEPM), Tulsa, Oklahoma, USA.

Ditton, R. B., and J. H. Gramann. 1987. A survey of down-island visitors and their use patterns at Padre Island National Seashore. Cooperative Park Study Unit Technical Report 6. Texas A&M University, Department of Recreation and Parks, Corpus Christi, Texas, USA.

Drawe, D. L. 1990. Succession of vegetation on Padre Island National Seashore. Progress report. Welder Wildlife Foundation, Sinton, Texas, USA.

Drawe, D. L., and I. M. Ortega. 1996. Impacts of geophysical seismic survey vehicles on Padre Island national seashore vegetation. Texas Journal of Science 48(2):107–118.

Echols, D., and E. Kassman. 2004. Regulations help endangered sea turtles make a comeback. Pages 92–93 in J. Selleck, editor. Natural Resource Year in

Review—2003. Technical Information Center (TIC) publication number D-1533. National Park Service, Denver, Colorado, and Washington, D.C., USA.

Fisk, H. N. 1959. Padre Island and the Laguna Madre flats, coastal South Texas. Pages 103–151 in R. J. Russell, editor. Proceedings of the 2nd Coastal Geography Conference, Louisiana State University, Baton Rouge, Louisiana, April 6–9, 1959. National Academy of Sciences, Washington, D.C., USA.

Gibbs, A. E., S. A. Cochran, J. B. Logan, and E. E. Grossman. 2007. Benthic habitats and offshore geological resources of Kaloko-Honnokōhau National Historical Park, Hawai'i. Scientific Investigations Report 2006-5256. U.S. Geological Survey, Reston, Virginia, USA.

Gibeaut, J., and T. Tremblay. 2005. Padre Island natural environments map (scale 1:5,000). Unpublished data. University of Texas, Bureau of Economic Geology, Austin, Texas, USA.

Godfrey, P. J. 1976. Management guidelines for parks and barrier beaches. U.S. Department of the Interior, National Park Service, Washington, D.C., USA.

Hart, L. 2003. Park Service names names in trashing Texas seashore. Online news article. Los Angeles Times (October 5, 2003). http://articles.latimes.com/2003/oct/05/nation/na-padre5 (accessed September 1, 2010).

Hayes, M. O. 1963. Grain size characteristics of Padre Island (Texas) sediments: A study of effects of bimodality on grain size parameters. The Texas Journal of Science 15:407–409.

Hayes, M. O. 1965. Sedimentation on a semiarid, wave-dominated coast (South Texas) with emphasis on hurricane effects. Dissertation. University of Texas, Austin, Texas, USA.

Hayes, M. O. 1967. Hurricanes as geologic agents: Case studies of Hurricane Carla, 1961, and Hurricane Cindy, 1963. Report of Investigations 61. University of Texas, Bureau of Economic Geology, Austin, Texas, USA.

Hill, G. W., and R. E. Hunter. 1976. Interaction of biological and geological processes in the beach and nearshore environments, northern Padre Island, Texas. Pages 169–187 in R. A. Davis Jr. and R. L. Ethington, editors. Beach and Nearshore Sedimentation. Special Publication 24. Society of Economic Paleontologists and Mineralogists (SEPM), Tulsa, Oklahoma, USA.

Hill, G. W., and R. E. Hunter. 1987. Interaction of biological and geological processes in the beach and nearshore environments, northern Padre Island, Texas. Pages 187–205 in R. A. Davis Jr., editor. Beach and Nearshore Sediments and Processes. Reprint

Series 12. Society of Economic Paleontologists and Mineralogists (SEPM), Tulsa, Oklahoma, USA.

Hunter, R. E. 1977. Basic types of stratification in small eolian dunes. Sedimentology 24:361–387.

Hunter, R. E., R. L. Watson, G. W. Hill, and K. A. Dickinson. 1972. Modern depositional environments and processes, northern and central Padre Island, Texas. Pages 1–27 in R. F. Travis, R. N. Tench, W. D. Hodgson, D. C. Callaway, and H. Wyneken, editors. Padre Island National Seashore Field Guide, GCAGS Convention Field Trip, October 14, 1972. Gulf Coast Association of Geological Societies, Corpus Christi, Texas, USA.

IPCC. 2007. Climate Change 2007: Synthesis Report. Contribution of Working Groups I, II and III to the Fourth Assessment Report of the Intergovernmental Panel on Climate Change. Intergovernmental Panel on Climate Change Geneva, Switzerland. http://www.ipcc.ch/publications_and_data/ar4/syr/en/contents.html. Accessed 9 September 2010.)

The John G & Marie Stella Kenedy Memorial Foundation. 2008. Kenedy Ranch overview. Online information. The John G & Marie Stella Kenedy Memorial Foundation, Corpus Christi, Texas, USA. http://www.kenedy.org/KenedyRanch/tabid/1093/Default.aspx (accessed September 1, 2010).

Jones, W. D. 1999. Padre Island National Seashore: An administrative history. National Park Service, Austin, Texas, USA. http://www.nps.gov/history/history/online_books/pais/index.htm (accessed September 1, 2010).

Karl, T. R., Melillo, J. M., and Peterson, T. C., 2009, Global climate change impacts in the United States. Cambridge University Press, New York, New York, USA. http://www.globalchange.gov/publications/reports/scientific-assessments/us-impacts. (accessed September 9, 2010.)

Kattner, K. R. 1973. Secondary successional vegetation on Padre Island National Seashore, Texas. Texas A&M University, Kingsville, Texas, USA.

Kenworthy, J. P., V. L. Santucci, and C. C. Visaggi. 2007. Paleontological resource inventory and monitoring, Gulf Coast Network. Technical Information Center (TIC) publication number D-750. National Park Service, Lakewood, Colorado, USA.

Leatherman, S. P. 1988. Barrier island handbook. 3rd edition. Coastal Publications Series. The University of Maryland, Laboratory for Coastal Research, College Park, Maryland, USA.

Leatherwood, A. 2008. The handbook of Texas online: Port Mansfield Channel. The Texas State Historical Association, Denton, Texas, USA. http://www.tshaonline.org/handbook/online/articles/PP/rup2.html (accessed September 1, 2010).

Lonard, R. I., F. W. Judd, J. H. Everitt, D. E. Escobar, M. A. Alaniz, I. Cavazos, and M. R. Davis. 1999. Vegetative change on South Padre Island, Texas, over twenty years and evaluation of multispectral videography in determining vegetative cover and species identity. Southwestern Naturalist 44:261–271.

Lundelius, E. L. Jr. 1972. Fossil vertebrates from the late Pleistocene Ingleside fauna, San Patricio County, Texas. Report of Investigations 77. University of Texas, Bureau of Economic Geology, Austin, Texas, USA.

Masson, P. H. 1955. An occurrence of gypsum in southwest Texas. Journal of Sedimentary Petrology 25:72–79.

McAtee, J. W. 1975. Human impact on the vegetation and microclimate on the beach and foredunes of Padre Island National Seashore. Thesis. Texas A&I University, Kingsville, Texas, USA.

McAtee, J. W., and D. L. Drawe. 1980. Human impact on beach and foredune vegetation on North Padre Island, Texas. Environmental Management 4(6):527–538.

McAtee, J. W., and D. L. Drawe. 1981. Human impact on beach and foredune microclimate on North Padre Island, Texas. Environmental Management 5(2):121–134.

McBride, E. F., and H. Honda. 1994. Carbonate sediments in shallowly buried Pleistocene and Holocene sandstone and limestone, South Texas gulf coast. Transactions of the Gulf Coast Association of Geological Societies 44:467–476.

McBride, E. F., H. Honda, and A. A. Abdel-Wahab. 1991. Fabric and origin of gypsum sand crystals, Laguna Madre, Texas. Abstract. AAPG Bulletin 75(9):1532.

McCoy, C. 2009. Protecting parks while achieving energy independence. Earth, Wind, & Water 2(4):1, 6–7. http://www1.nrintra.nps.gov/nrpc/newsletters/pdf/2009/NRPCNewsSpring_2009.pdf (NPS intranet access only, August 28, 2009).

McGowen, J. H., L. F. Brown Jr., T. R. Calnan, J. L. Chin, J. P. Herber, and C. L. Lewis. 1977. History and processes involved in development of South Padre Island, Laguna Madre, and Los Bancos de en Medio. Report to Texas General Land Office. University of Texas, Bureau of Economic Geology, Austin, Texas, USA.

McGowen, J. H., C. G. Groat, L. F. Brown Jr., W. L. Fisher, and A. J. Scott. 1970. Effects of Hurricane Celia: A focus on environmental geologic problems of the Texas coastal zone. Circular 70-3. University of Texas, Bureau of Economic Geology, Austin, Texas, USA.

McGowen, J. H., C. V. Proctor, L. F. Brown Jr., T. H. Evans, W. L. Fisher, and C. G. Groat. 1976.

Environmental geologic atlas of the Texas coastal zone: Port Lavaca area. University of Texas, Bureau of Economic Geology, Austin, Texas, USA.

McGowen, J. H., and A. J. Scott. 1975. Hurricanes and geologic agents on the Texas coast. Pages 23–43 *in* Estuarine Research. Volume 2: Geology and Engineering. Academic Press, New York, New York, USA.

Meehl, G. A., Stocker, T. F., Collins, W. D., Friedlingstein, P., Gaye, A. T., Gregory, J. M., Kitoh, A., Knutti, R., Murphy, J. M., Noda, A., Raper, S. C. B., Watterson, I. G., J, W. A., and Zhao, Z.-C. 2007. Global Climate Projections. *in* S. Solomon, D. Qin, M. Manning, Z. Chen, M. Marquis, K. B. Averyt, M. Tignor, and H. L. Miller, editors. Climate Change 2007: The Physical Science Basis. Contribution of Working Group I to the Fourth Assessment Report of the Intergovernmental Panel on Climate Change. Cambridge University Press, Cambridge, United Kingdom and New York, New York, USA. http://www.ipcc-wg1.unibe.ch/publications/wg1-ar4/wg1-ar4.html (accessed September 9, 2010).

Miller, G. W., and R. E. Hunter. 1979. Distribution of macroinvertebrates from subsurface Quaternary shell beds, northern Padre Island, Texas. Open-File Report OFR 79-1324. U.S. Geological Survey, Reston, Virginia, USA.

Miller, J. E., and E. R. Jones. 2003. Shoreline trash: Studies at Padre Island National Seashore, 1989–1998. Padre Island National Seashore and Texas A&M University, Corpus Christi, Texas, USA.

Morton, R. A. 1977. Historical shoreline changes and their causes, Texas gulf coast. Gulf Coast Association of Geological Societies Transactions 27:352–364.

Morton, R. A. 1994. Texas barriers. Pages 75–114 *in* R. A. Davis, editor. Geology of Holocene Barrier Islands. Springer-Verlag, Berlin, Germany.

Morton, R. A. 2003. An overview of coastal land loss with emphasis on the southeastern United States. Open-File Report 2003-337. U.S. Geological Survey, Center for Coastal and Watershed Studies, St. Petersburg, Florida, USA.

Morton, R. A., and C. W. Holmes. 2009. Geological processes and sedimentation rates of wind-tidal flats, Laguna Madre, Texas. Gulf Coast Association of Geological Societies Transactions 59:519–538.

Morton, R. A., and J. H. McGowen. 1980. Modern depositional environments of the Texas coast. Guidebook 20. University of Texas, Bureau of Economic Geology, Austin, Texas, USA.

Morton, R. A., T. L. Miller, and L. J. Moore. 2004. National assessment of shorelines change: Part 1—Historical shoreline changes and associated coastal land loss along the U.S. Gulf of Mexico. Open-File

Report 2004-1043. U.S. Geological Survey, Center for Coastal and Watershed Studies, St. Petersburg, Florida, USA.

Morton, R. A., and J. G. Paine. 1985. Beach and vegetation-line changes at Galveston Island, Texas: Erosion, deposition, and recovery from Hurricane Alicia. Geological Circular 85-5. University of Texas, Bureau of Economic Geology, Austin, Texas, USA.

Morton, R. A., and W. A. Price. 1987. Late Quaternary sea-level fluctuations and sedimentary phases of the Texas coastal plain and shelf. Pages 181–198 *in* D. Nummedal, O. H. Pilkey, and J. D. Howard, editors. Sea Level Fluctuations and Coastal Evolution. Special Publication 41. Society of Economic Paleontologists and Mineralogists (SEPM), Tulsa, Oklahoma, USA.

Morton, R. A., and F. M. Speed. 1998. Evaluation of shorelines and legal boundaries controlled by water levels on sandy beaches. Journal of Coastal Research 14(4):1373–1384.

National Park Service. 1973. Master plan, Padre Island National Seashore, Texas. U.S. Department of the Interior, National Park Service, Denver Service Center, Denver, Colorado, USA.

National Park Service. 1994. Padre Island National Seashore statement for interpretation. Padre Island National Seashore, Corpus Christi, Texas, USA.

National Park Service. 1995. Padre Island National Seashore parkwide development concept plan and environmental assessment. Public draft (January 2005). Technical Information Center (TIC) publication number D-58. Padre Island National Seashore, Corpus Christi, Texas, USA.

National Park Service. 2000. Final oil and gas management plan / environmental impact statement, February 2000, Padre Island National Seashore, Klegberg, Kenedy, and Willacy counties, Texas. U.S. Department of the Interior, National Park Service, Corpus Christi, Texas, USA.

National Park Service. 2001. Management policies 2001. NPS D1416 (December 2000). U.S. Department of the Interior, National Park Service, Washington, D.C., USA.

National Park Service. 2006a. Management policies 2006. U.S. Department of the Interior, National Park Service, Washington, D.C., USA.

National Park Service. 2006b. Padre Island National Seashore: Coasts / Shorelines. Online information. Padre Island National Seashore, Corpus Christi, Texas, USA. http://www.nps.gov/pais/naturescience/coasts.htm (accessed September 1, 2010).

National Park Service. 2006c. Padre Island National Seashore: Mollusks. Online information. Padre Island National Seashore, Corpus Christi, Texas, USA.

http://www.nps.gov/pais/naturescience/coasts.htm (accessed September 1, 2010).

National Park Service. 2006d. Padre Island National Seashore: The oil and gas program at Padre Island National Seashore. Online information. Padre Island National Seashore, Corpus Christi, Texas, USA. http://www.nps.gov/pais/parkmgmt/white-paper.htm (accessed September 1, 2010).

National Park Service. 2007. Padre Island National Seashore: Geologic formations. Online information. Padre Island National Seashore, Corpus Christi, Texas, USA. http://www.nps.gov/pais/naturescience/geologicformations.htm (accessed September 2, 2010).

National Park Service. 2009. Padre Island National Seashore: History & culture. Online information. Padre Island National Seashore, Corpus Christi, Texas, USA. http://www.nps.gov/pais/historyculture/index.htm (accessed August 30, 2010).

National Park Service. 2010a. Explore nature: Explore geology. Coastal geology in our national parks: Global climate change and sea-level rise. Online information. http://www.nature.nps.gov/geology/coastal/gw_slr.cfm (accessed September 2, 2010).

National Park Service. 2010b. Padre Island National Seashore: Bird Island Basin. Online information. Padre Island National Seashore, Corpus Christi, Texas, USA. http://www.nps.gov/pais/planyourvisit/bird_island_basin.htm (accessed August 31, 2010).

Norby, L. 2008. Updated reasonably foreseeable development scenario for oil and gas development at Padre Island National Seashore, October 31, 2008. National Park Service, Geologic Resources Division, Denver, Colorado, USA.

Nummedal, D., S. Penland, R. Gerdes, W. Schram, J. Kahn, and H. Roberts. 1980. Geologic response of hurricane impact on low-profile gulf coast barriers. Gulf Coast Association of Geological Societies Transactions 30:183–195.

Parry, M. L., O. F. Canziani, J. P. Palutikof, P. J. van der Linden, and C. E. Hanson. 2007. Climate Change 2007: Impacts, adaptation and vulnerability. Contribution of Working Group II to the Fourth Assessment Report of the Intergovernmental Panel on Climate Change (IPCC). Cambridge University Press, Cambridge, United Kingdom, and New York, New Yor, USA. http://www.ipcc-wg2.org/ (accessed September 1, 2010).

Pendleton, E. A., R. Thieler, S. J. Williams, and R. L. Beavers. 2004. Coastal vulnerability assessment of Padre Island National Seashore (PAIS) to sea-level rise. Open-File Report 2004-1090. U.S. Geological Survey, Reston, Virginia, USA.

Pinet, P. R. 1992. Oceanography: An introduction to the planet oceanus. West Publishing Company, St. Paul, Minnesota, USA.

Price, W. A. 1958. Sedimentology and Quaternary geomorphology of South Texas. Gulf Coast Association of Geological Societies Transactions 8:41–75.

Price, W. A. 1987. Range cattle, critical factor in eolian plain stabilization. Abstract. Page 67 in SEPM Annual Midyear Meeting, Volume 4. Society of Economic Paleontologists and Mineralogists (SEPM), Tulsa, Oklahoma, USA.

Price, W. A., and G. Gunter. 1942. Certain recent and geological and biological changes to South Texas, with consideration of probable causes. Texas Academy of Science Proceedings and Transactions 26:138–156.

Prouty, J. S. 1989. Historical back-barrier shoreline changes, Padre Island National Seashore, Texas. Abstract. AAPG Bulletin 73(9):1190.

Rabalais, N. N. 1977. Gulf beach national environmental study area. Padre Island National Seashore, Corpus Christi, Texas, USA.

Rahmstorf, S. 2007. A semi-empirical approach to projecting future sea-level rise. Science 315:368–370.

Roth, D. 2004. Texas hurricane history: Featured storm—Bret (1999). National Weather Service, Lake Charles, Louisiana, USA.

Roth, D. 2009. Texas hurricane history. Online document. National Weather Service, Camp Springs, Maryland, USA. http://www.hpc.ncep.noaa.gov/research/txhur.pdf (accessed September 1, 2010).

Rusnak, G. A. 1960. Sediment of the Laguna Madre. Pages 153–196 in F. P. Shepherd, F. B. Phelger, and T. J. van Andel, editors. Recent Sediments, Northwestern Gulf of Mexico. American Association of Petroleum Geologists, Tulsa, Oklahoma, USA.

Scott, A. J., Hoover, R. A., and McGowen, J. H. 1969. Effects of Hurricane Beulah, 1967, on Texas coastal lagoons and barriers. Pages 221–236 in A. A. Castañares, F. B. Phleger, and D. F. México, editors. Lagunas Costeras: Un Simposio. UNAM-UNESCO, Memorandum Simposio Internacional Lagunas Costeras. Universidad Nacional Autónoma de México, Mexico City, Mexico.

Sheire, J. W. 1971. Padre Island National Seashore historic resource study. Technical Information Center (TIC) publication number D-1. U.S. Department of the Interior, National Park Service, Office of History and Historic Architecture, Washington, D.C., USA.

Smith-Engle, J. M., R. G. Hay, and D. D. Williams. 2006. Padre Island National Seashore, Bird Island Basin beach restoration project—Phase one. Final report.

Texas A&M University, College of Science and Technology, Corpus Christi, Texas, USA.

Smith-Engle, J. M., R. Hay, and D. Williams. 2007. Models for beach renourishment of a back-barrier shoreline, Padre Island National Seashore, Texas. Gulf Coast Association of Geological Societies Transactions 57:679–683.

Suter, J. R., and A. K. Maynard. 1983. Regional variability of washover deposits on South Texas coast. Abstract. AAPG Bulletin 67(9):1473.

Teerling, J. 1970. The incidence of the ghost crab *Ocypode quadrata* (Fabr) on the forebeach of Padre Island, and some of its responses to man. Thesis. Texas A&I University, Kingsville, Texas, USA.

Texas Center for Policy Studies. 2001. The Gulf Intracoastal Waterway from Corpus Christi to Brownsville: Little value, big cost. An update to the 1994 report: "Subsidized destruction." Online document. Texas Center for Policy Studies, Austin, Texas, USA. http://www.texascenter.org/publications/littlevaluebigcost.pdf (accessed September 2, 2010).

Thayer, P. A., A. La Rocque, and J. W. Tunnell Jr. 1974. Relict lacustrine sediments on the inner continental shelf, southeast Texas. Gulf Coast Association of Geological Societies Transactions 24:337–347.

Tunnell, J. W. Jr. 2002a. Geography, climate, and hydrology. Pages 7–27 *in* J. W. Tunnell Jr. and F. W. Judd, editors. The Laguna Madre of Texas and Tamaulipas. Texas A&M University Press, College Station, Texas, USA.

Tunnell, J. W. Jr. 2002b. Origin, development, and geology. Pages 28–37 *in* J. W. Tunnell Jr. and F. W. Judd, editors. The Laguna Madre of Texas and Tamaulipas. Texas A&M University Press, College Station, Texas, USA.

Tunnell, J. W. Jr., K. Withers, and E. H. Smith. 2002. Conservation issues and recommendations. Pages 275–288 *in* J. W. Tunnell, Jr. and F. W. Judd, editors. The Laguna Madre of Texas and Tamaulipas. Texas A&M University, College Station, Texas, USA.

U.S. Army Corps of Engineers. 2003. Final environmental impact statement, Volume 1: Maintenance dredging of the Gulf Intracoastal Waterway Laguna Madre, Texas, Nueces, Kleberg, Kenedy, Willacy, and Cameron counties, Texas (September 2003). U.S. Army Corps of Engineers, Galveston District, Southwestern Division, Galveston, Texas, USA. http://www.swg.usace.army.mil/items/Laguna/eis/Laguna%20Madre%20FEIS%20-%20Volume%20I.pdf (accessed September 2, 2010).

U.S. Army Corps of Engineers. 2005. Laguna Madre project. Online information. U.S. Army Corps of Engineers, Galveston District, Galveston, Texas, USA.

http://www.swg.usace.army.mil/items/Laguna/special_studies/ (accessed September 2, 2010).

U.S. Geological Survey. 2008. Coastal change hazards: Hurricanes and extreme storms. Hurricane Ike: Initial assessment of potential coastal-change impacts. Online information. U.S. Geological Survey, St. Petersburg, Florida, USA. http://coastal.er.usgs.gov/hurricanes/ike/coastal-change/ (accessed September 2, 2010).

van Andel, T. H. 1960. Sources and dispersion of Holocene sediments, northern Gulf of Mexico. Pages 34–55 *in* F. P. Shepard, F. B. Phleger, and T. H. van Andel, editors. Recent Sediments, Northwest Gulf of Mexico. American Association of Petroleum Geologists (AAPG), Tulsa, Oklahoma, USA.

Watson, R. L. 1968. Origin of shell beaches, Padre Island, Texas. Thesis. University of Texas, Austin, Texas, USA.

Weise, B. R., and W. A. White. 1980. Padre Island National Seashore: A guide to the geology, natural environments, and history of a Texas barrier island. Guidebook 17. University of Texas, Bureau of Economic Geology, Austin, Texas, USA.

Wicksten, M. K., T. M. Green, and M. H. Sweet. 1987. A quantitative study of sandy beach organisms at Padre Island National Seashore. Texas A&M University, Department of Biology, College Station, Texas, USA.

Withers, K. 1996. An evaluation of recovery of benthic invertebrate communities in vehicle tracks and restored oil and gas impacted areas on wind-tidal flats in the upper Laguna Madre, Padre Island National Seashore, Texas. Contract 1443PX749050162. U.S. Department of the Interior, National Park Service, Natural Resource Program Center, Water Resources Division, Fort Collins, Colorado, USA..

Withers, K., E. Smith, O. Romez, and J. Wood. 2004. Assessment of coastal water resources and watershed conditions at Padre Island National Seashore, Texas. Technical Report NPS/NRWRD/WRTR—2004/323. U.S. Department of the Interior, National Park Service, Natural Resource Program Center, Water Resources Division, Fort Collins, Colorado, USA.

Zervas, C. 2001. Sea level variations of the United States 1854–1999. Technical Report NOS CO-OPS 36. National Oceanographic and Atmospheric Administration (NOAA), Silver Spring, Maryland, USA. http://tidesandcurrents.noaa.gov/publications/techrpt36doc.pdf (accessed September 2, 2010).

Additional References

This section lists additional references, resources, and web sites that may be of use to resource managers. Web addresses are current as of September 2010

Geology of National Park Service Areas

National Park Service Geologic Resources Division (Lakewood, Colorado): http://nature.nps.gov/geology/

NPS Geologic Resources Inventory: http://www.nature.nps.gov/geology/inventory/gre_publications.cfm

U.S. Geological Survey Geology of National Parks (includes 3D photographs): http://3dparks.wr.usgs.gov/

Harris, A. G., E. Tuttle, and S. D. Tuttle. 2003. Geology of National Parks. Sixth Edition. Kendall/Hunt Publishing Co., Dubuque, Iowa, USA.

Kiver, E. P. and D. V. Harris. 1999. Geology of U.S. parklands. John Wiley and Sons, Inc., New York, New York, USA.

Lillie, R. J. 2005. Parks and Plates: The geology of our national parks, monuments, and seashores. W.W. Norton and Co., New York, New York, USA. [Geared for interpreters].

NPS Geoscientist-in-the-parks (GIP) internship and guest scientist program: http://www.nature.nps.gov/geology/gip/index.cfm

Resource Management/Legislation Documents

NPS 2006 Management Policies (Chapter 4; Natural Resource Management): http://www.nps.gov/policy/mp/policies.html

NPS-75: Natural Resource Inventory and Monitoring Guideline: http://www.nature.nps.gov/nps75/nps75.pdf.

NPS Natural Resource Management Reference Manual #77: http://www.nature.nps.gov/Rm77/

Geologic Monitoring Manual
  R. Young and L. Norby, editors. Geological Monitoring. Geological Society of America, Boulder, Colorado.

  [Website under development]. Contact the Geologic Resources Division to obtain a copy.

NPS Technical Information Center (Denver, repository for technical (TIC) documents): http://etic.nps.gov/

National Park Service Climate Change

National Park Service Climate Change Response Program: http://www.nature.nps.gov/climatechange/index.cfm

Global climate change impacts in the United States report (Karl et al. 2009) http://www.globalchange.gov/publications/reports/scientific-assessments/us-impacts.

Geological Survey Websites

Texas Bureau of Economic Geology http://www.beg.utexas.edu/

U.S. Geological Survey: http://www.usgs.gov/

Geological Society of America: http://www.geosociety.org/

American Geological Institute: http://www.agiweb.org/ Association of American State Geologists: http://www.stategeologists.org/

Other Geology/Resource Management Tools

Bates, R. L. and J. A. Jackson, editors. American Geological Institute dictionary of geological terms (3rd Edition). Bantam Doubleday Dell Publishing Group, New York.

U.S. Geological Survey National Geologic Map Database (NGMDB): http://ngmdb.usgs.gov/

U.S. Geological Survey Geologic Names Lexicon (GEOLEX; geologic unit nomenclature and summary): http://ngmdb.usgs.gov/Geolex/geolex_home.html

U.S. Geological Survey Geographic Names Information System (GNIS; search for place names and geographic features, and plot them on topographic maps or aerial photos): http://gnis.usgs.gov/

U.S. Geological Survey GeoPDFs (download searchable PDFs of any topographic map in the United States): http://store.usgs.gov (click on "Map Locator").

U.S. Geological Survey Publications Warehouse (many USGS publications are available online): http://pubs.usgs.gov

U.S. Geological Survey, description of physiographic provinces: http://tapestry.usgs.gov/Default.html

Appendix A: Overview of Digital Geologic Data

The following pages are an overview of the digital geologic data for Padre Island National Seashore. For poster-size PDFs of this overview and complete digital data, please see the included CD or visit the Geologic Resources Inventory publications web site: http://www.nature.nps.gov/geology/inventory/gre_publications.cfm.

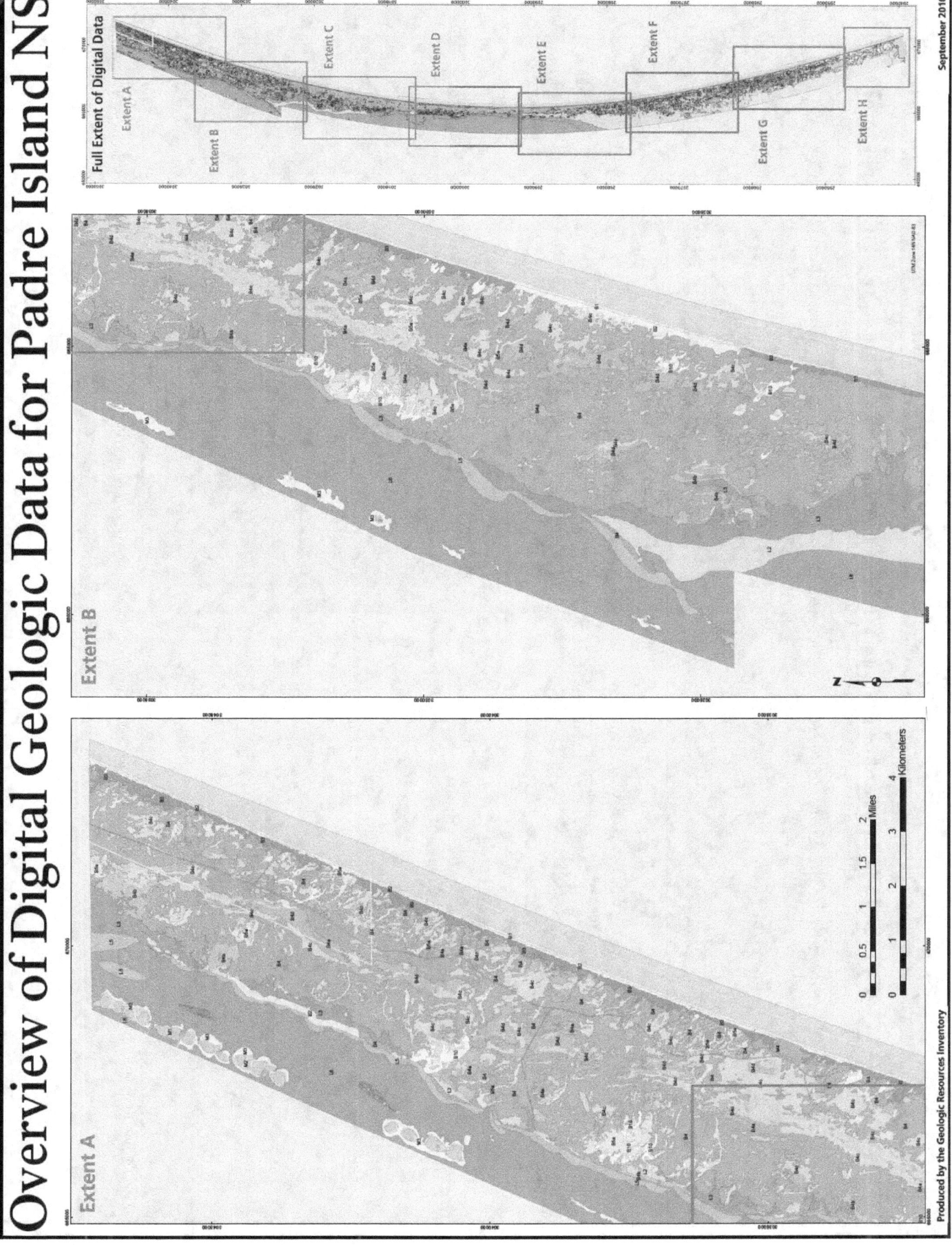

Overview of Digital Geologic Data for Padre Island NS

Full Extent of Digital Data

Extent A
Extent B
Extent C
Extent D
Extent E
Extent F
Extent G
Extent H

Extent B

Extent A

Produced by the Geologic Resources Inventory

September 2010

Padre Island National Seashore
Texas

National Park Service
U.S. Department of the Interior

Overview of Digital Geologic Data for Padre Island NS

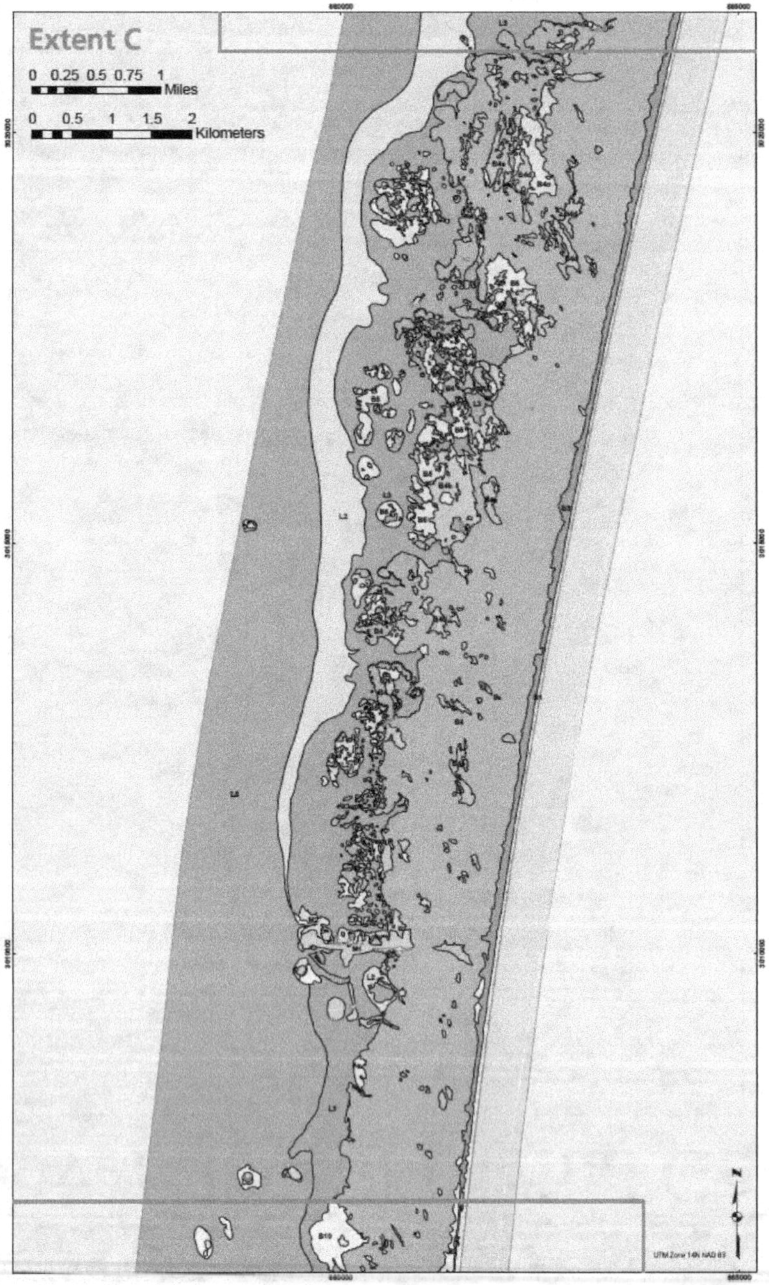
Extent C
0 0.25 0.5 0.75 1 Miles
0 0.5 1 1.5 2 Kilometers
UTM Zone 14N NAD 83

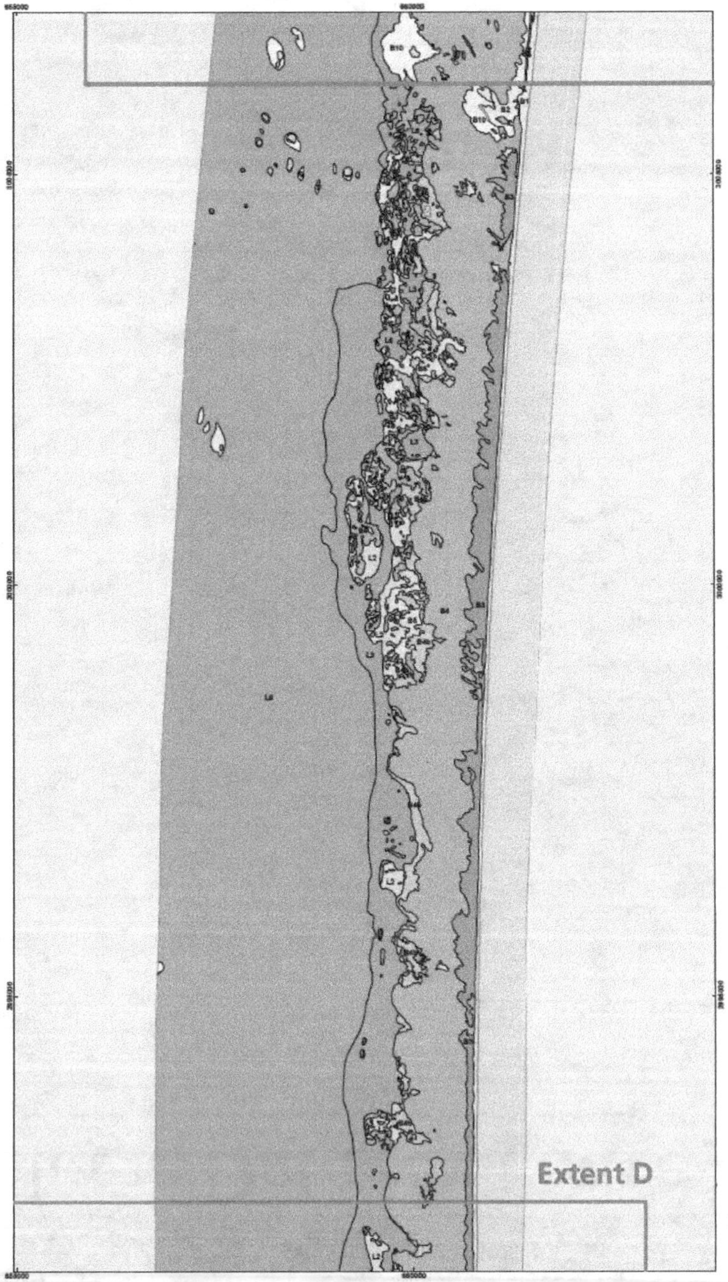
Extent D

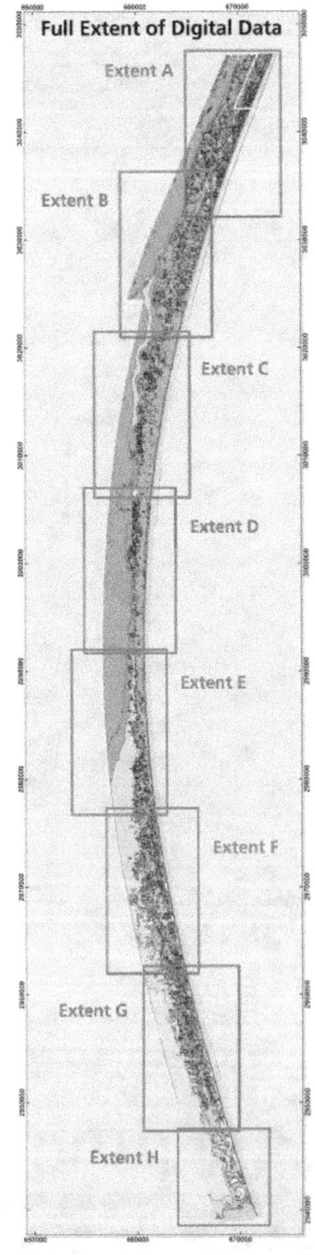
Full Extent of Digital Data
Extent A
Extent B
Extent C
Extent D
Extent E
Extent F
Extent G
Extent H

Produced by the Geologic Resources Inventory

September 2010

Overview of Digital Geologic Data for Padre Island NS

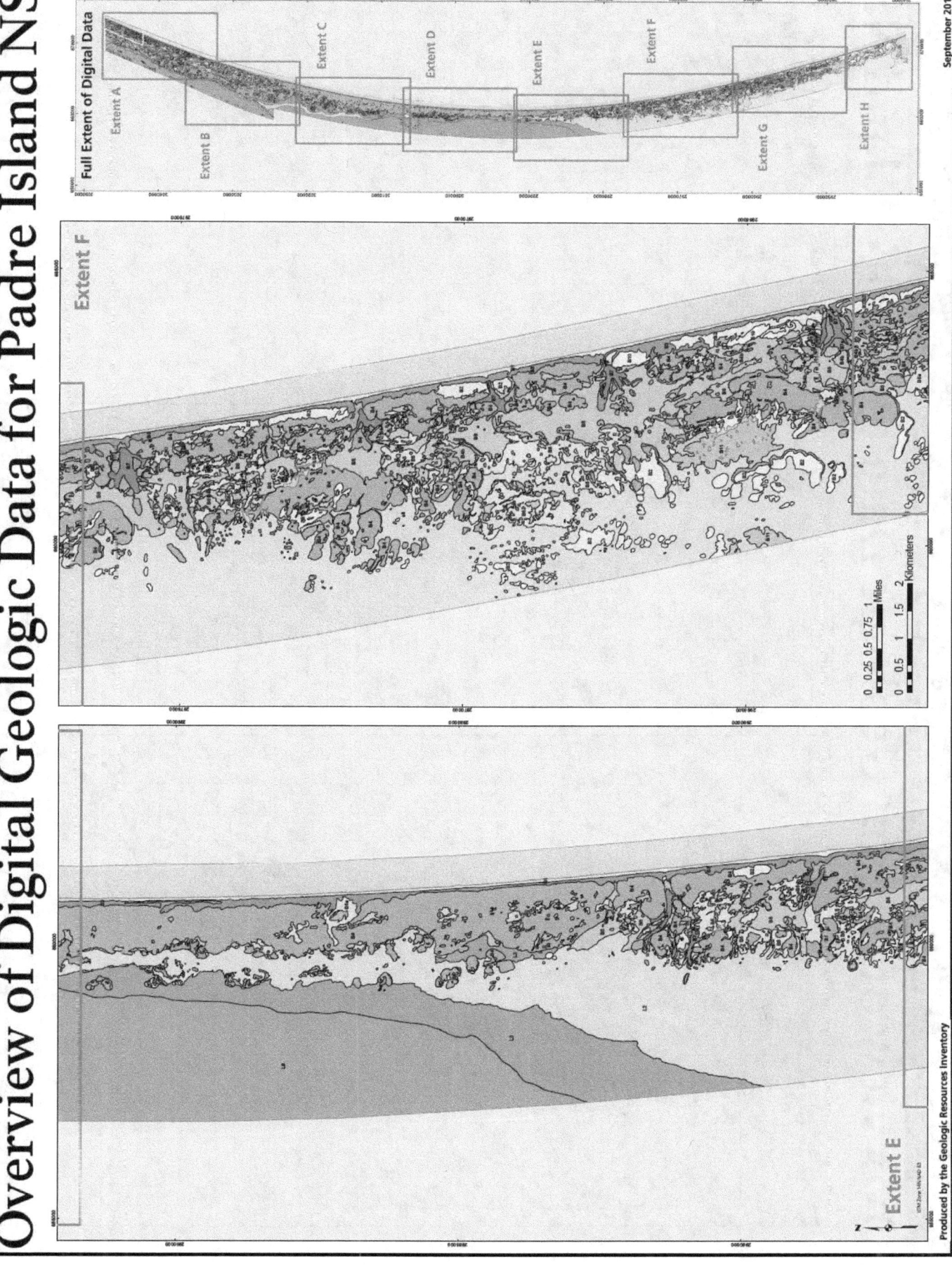

Full Extent of Digital Data

Extent A
Extent B
Extent C
Extent D
Extent E
Extent F
Extent G
Extent H

Extent F

Extent E

Miles
0 0.25 0.5 0.75 1

Kilometers
0 0.5 1 1.5 2

September 2010

Produced by the Geologic Resources Inventory

Overview of Digital Geologic Data for Padre Island NS

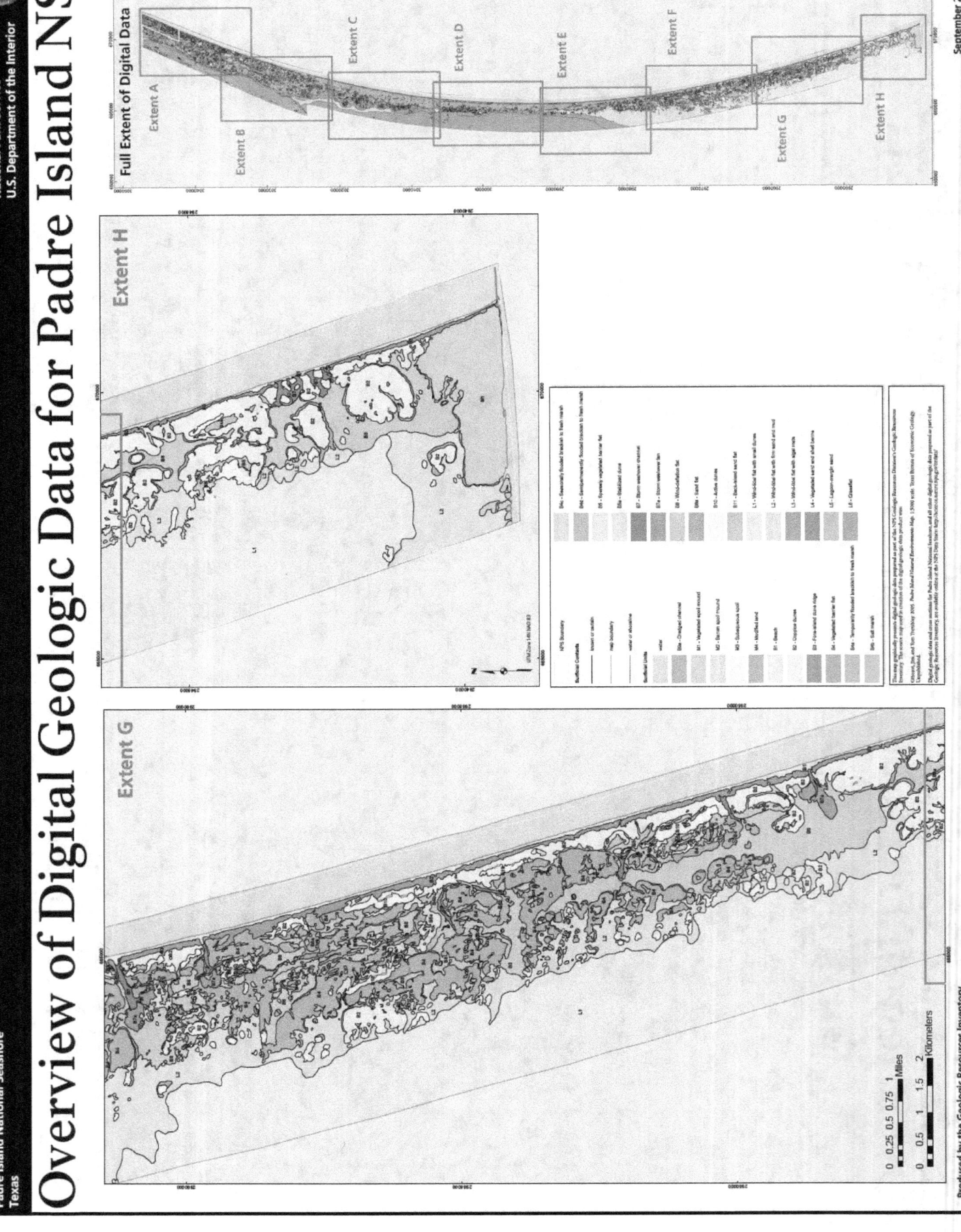

September 2010

NPS 613/105619, September 2010

www.ingramcontent.com/pod-product-compliance
Lightning Source LLC
Chambersburg PA
CBHW080907290526
45795CB00007BA/2442